TAKING OFF

EXTRAORDINARY WAYS TO SPEND YOUR FIRST YEAR OUT OF COLLEGE

OFF

LAUREN TARSHIS

A FIRESIDE BOOK
NEW YORK · LONDON · TORONTO · SYDNEY ·
TOKYO

FIRESIDE
SIMON & SCHUSTER BUILDING
ROCKEFELLER CENTER
1230 AVENUE OF THE AMERICAS
NEW YORK, NEW YORK 10020

FIRESIDE AND COLOPHON ARE REGISTERED TRADEMARKS
OF SIMON & SCHUSTER INC.

DESIGNED BY DIANE STEVENSON/SNAP•HAUS GRAPHICS

MANUFACTURED IN THE UNITED STATES OF AMERICA

3   5   7   9   10   8   6   4

LIBRARY OF CONGRESS CATALOGING IN PUBLICATION DATA

ISBN 0-671-67193-6

ACKNOWLEDGMENTS

I would like to thank the hundreds of people whose information, inspiration, and support helped me write this book. There are a few who deserve special mention: Patty Brown, Tim McGinnis, and Cindy Lao for helping me shape my idea into a book; Andrew Tarshis, Cathy Lewis, Laura Viederman, and Suzanne Gerber for their honesty and good advice; Joanne Comerford, Kevin Kelly, and Linda Molnar for catching my mistakes; and my husband, David, for his infinite love, wit, confidence, patience, computer wizardry, and medleys.

TO MY PARENTS

CONTENTS

INTRODUCTION 13

1 OPPORTUNITIES ABROAD

2 VOLUNTEER OPPORTUNITIES

3 OPPORTUNITIES IN THE OUTDOORS

4 FOR MORE INFORMATION

INTRODUCTION

During the spring semester of my senior year in college, I made up my mind that I wasn't ready to start a career. I felt that I had some more learning to do, not in graduate school, but in the world. I was happy about my decision, and set out to find the perfect experience—one that would challenge me, inspire me, and teach me something about life. I searched for about two months, spending hours in the career placement office of my college, in bookstores and libraries, talking to my friends and my parents. But I found nothing. I came up with lots of information about starting a career, but not very much on full-time volunteer opportunities, jobs overseas, and outdoor adventures—the kind of experiences that I was looking for. When I *did* find something intriguing, it required some kind of experience I didn't have, some language I didn't speak, some commitment I wasn't prepared to make, or sums of money that I couldn't pay.

So I gave up. I finished my exams, sat through graduation, moved back home, and was ensconced in my first post-graduate job within a couple of months. I don't regret having taken that job, but I've always felt that I missed out on something. Over the next few years I learned about dozens of wonderful opportunities open to recent graduates. I met people who lived and worked in China. I read about jobs in national parks, where you spend days leading nature tours or studying moose populations. I found out about a program that allows recent college graduates to work legally in such countries as France, England, Germany, and New Zealand. I talked to people who taught English in Kenya, worked with human rights activists in Guatemala, and hiked the Appalachian Trail.

I realized that there are many available opportunities out there, but for the average college senior, mired in schoolwork and confused (even traumatized) about the future, finding out about any one of them can be extremely difficult. This book will simplify the task. In an earlier time it would have led me to the challenging, broadening experience that I was looking for. Now it can do that for you.

Of the hundreds of opportunities I uncovered in my research, I focused on those that are especially suited for someone just out of college, based on conversations I had with recent graduates who have lived through each experience. Nearly all of these experiences offer some kind of financial support: usually room, board, and a small stipend. You won't get rich, but neither will you have to worry much about supporting yourself along the way. Also, most programs are tied to some sort of umbrella organization, an entity that will help you while you are getting involved or if there should be a problem down the line.

What you will get out of one of these experiences depends on your goals, how you approach them, and what sort of person you are. For some people, a year off is simply an interesting diversion from a set plan, a chance to learn about themselves and the world and to confront challenges different from those related to college or work.

Kevin, for instance, who majored in urban studies in college, headed into the Peace Corps right after graduation. He spent nearly three years in Costa Rica, consulting with owners of small businesses, building clay ovens in remote villages, and working with orphans. Within a few months of his return to New York, however, he had landed a job with the planning department of the Transit Authority, a goal he had set during his junior year in college.

Others, though, are like Tina, whose life course was irreversibly altered by her experience at Camphill Special Schools, a residential school for mentally handicapped children. "I came to Camphill because I was looking for something worthwhile to do after college," she says, still working as a volunteer 17 years later. "But I fell in love with the kids and I couldn't leave. I got married here and now I have three of my own kids."

For still other graduates, a year off is a time to test the waters of a possible career—in ecology, diplomacy, overseas development, teaching, medicine—and to get the kind of hands-on experience that will lead to a first job. Most major overseas relief agencies, like Save the Children, Concern, and Catholic Relief Services, consider a stint in the Peace Corps or similar volunteer organization a prerequisite to a career-track job.

Which brings up one of the major issues relating to time off after college—its effect on future job prospects. Employers have varying perspectives and policies, but the bottom line, according to some experts, career counselors, and personnel executives I've spoken with, is best summed up by a recruiter for a major investment banking firm: "It's a great advantage if you can come into an interview and say 'I'm an interesting person and here's why.' We get hundreds of applications a week, so if you've done something during a year off that sets you apart as a risk taker, as someone who pushes yourself past your boundaries, it's better than having worked a summer in Joe Doe's investment company in the middle of nowhere."

The listings in this book present an honest picture of each experience, and the kind of information you need to figure out if it's something you would like to do. I've included a wide range of opportunities, designed to appeal to many different types of people. And in reading through them, it's important that you keep your sights on personal goals, motivations, interests, and needs. Even the smallest factors, experienced recent graduates agree, can have an enormous impact on your experience. If you're squeamish about using gas station restrooms, for example, you might think twice about joining a program that takes place in a third world village. A bit of pragmatism won't squelch your sense of adventure. And it will make your experience more successful, both practically and spiritually. With these caveats in mind, I invite you to launch what could well be one of the most meaningful experiences of your life.

OPPORTUNITIES ABROAD

CHAPTER ONE

T he best way to start planning to live and work abroad is by clearing your mind of any negative rumors you might have heard regarding your prospects. Despite widespread beliefs, many jobs and volunteer positions are available. You *don't* need to speak another language. You *don't* need a unique skill. And you *don't* need high-ranking contacts.

The jobs and volunteer positions listed in this chapter are open to virtually any recent graduate. And though you won't make your fortune in them, you should be able to cover basic expenses and usually some travel costs as well. You will also get to know another country as a real participant, living alongside the inhabitants, following the customs, and avoiding the mistaken impressions we often get as tourists.

Anyone who has lived in Israel, for example, knows how quickly the legendary Israeli pushiness ("There are old women shoving you on buses") gives way to warmth and hospitality. "Whenever you go to somebody's house, they want to feed you and offer you a shower, even if they have just met you," says Andrew, who spent a year in Israel following graduation.

The most interesting aspect of living abroad, experienced graduates agree, is not just what you learn about the country, but what you learn about yourself. You are exposed to a whole new set of priorities—material priorities, professional priorities, and spiritual priorities. At the same time, you are removed from the points of reference that have shaped your own values—your family and friends. Russell, who spent time in Japan during college, comments, "Most people who live overseas, especially at that stage of their lives, have some sort of seminal experience, a moment of conversion. It might must be something funny or out of the ordinary that occurs. But it gives them insight."

This insight might be as straightforward as a new career goal, or so far-reaching that it completely changes the way you approach life. Few people remain unaffected, however. "I realized that I can live simply," says another Russell, who spent more than a year teaching in China. "I lived in a dorm with no hot water and heat. Shopping and traveling short distances took hours. People tell me [now] that I must realize how great all the luxuries in America are. But I say that I realize how unnecessary they are."

The opportunities in this chapter include both regular jobs and expense-paid volunteer positions. If you are thinking about the volunteer route, you should read through the introduction to Chapter 2, Volunteer Opportunities, beginning on page 117. You should not commit to a volunteer position simply because you want to live overseas; while the cultural dimension of living in a foreign country will have a strong impact on your volunteer experience, your first priority should be the work itself. "We're not here to support people' travels in Asia and Chinese language education," says Carolyn, a former volunteer coordinator for the YMCA's Overseas Corps in Taiwan. "We're a volunteer organization."

I have not included any specific listings about short-term jobs overseas, such as picking fruit in France and temporary employment in Australia. These jobs are a great boost for people trying to subsidize long trips, but unfortunately you can't arrange them in advance. Most travelers hear about openings from other travelers and are hired on the spot. So it's difficult to offer much in the way of planning advice.

As for visas, immunizations, and other preparations, each country has different policies which your program director will tell you about. At the end of some listings, though, I have recommended a few travel and culture books that will help if you are making your own arrangements.

CHINA

TEACHING ENGLISH IN A CHINESE UNIVERSITY

Recent graduates who have taught English in Chinese universities marvel over the personal rewards, the travel, and the learning opportunities. But more than anything else, it seems, they love to tell stories about their encounters with a culture that has little in common with their own. Dan, who taught for two years at an architectural college near the Sichuan city of Chongqing, especially likes to tell about the Beijing hotel where he spent his first night in China. "Like some American hotels, the bathroom was stocked with a tube of toothpaste and a toothbrush," he says, "except the toothbrush that they left for me had been used." Stacy, who spent a year teaching at the Sichuan Institute of Finance and Economics in Chengdu, recalls with some relish her experience with Chinese bluntness.

"They asked me why I was so fat," she says, her rather slim figure seated at a desk at New York's China Institute, where she now works. "And then they asked me if my mother is as fat as I am."

The repertoire of these stories is endless, and their protagonists repeat them with a mixture of good humor and lingering shock—which, in large part, characterizes the American experience in China.

Despite the influx of tourists, students, and scholars into China since 1979, China's door is still just inching open. And in many instances, the Chinese are less than sure of what to make of foreigners, especially Westerners. This means that you will bang heads with a bureaucracy that is astoundingly tangled and inefficient, especially when dealing with foreigners. "If you need something, even a piece of information, and the one person in charge doesn't want to give it to you or isn't around, there is no one else who will give it to you," says Dan.

But for most American teachers, being a trailblazer translates into a remarkably fresh experience. A western face is a novelty in many regions. And though you'll receive many stares (every American teacher knows the feeling of being followed through the market by 50 gaping Chinese), you will also be treated with great kindness and hospitality. Furthermore, you will have the chance to visit places that are largely untouched by tourists, areas that are unlike any you have ever seen or been able to imagine, and that reflect thousands of years of history.

The key to a successful experience in China, former teachers agree, is having a totally open mind, an ability to laugh, and unlimited reserves of calm. There is no place for American impatience in China. "Everything in China is completely different from America," says Russell, who spent a year teaching in Hubei Province. "It's like a cultural puzzle where you are constantly having to figure out what is going on."

As a recent graduate, your best (and only, as of this writing) job option is teaching English at a Chinese university. There are hundreds of universities in China, and many rely on foreigners to teach English. American English, for some reason, is the preferred variety. "They call it 'standard English,' " says Stacy.

You do not have to speak Chinese to get a teaching position, although even the most basic understanding of Chinese can make an enormous difference in your ability to participate in the culture. Former teachers strongly recommend taking an introductory course in Chinese beforehand and indulging all opportunities to practice it while you're in China. "If you don't know the language, you find yourself a passive observer because you can't interact," says Russell. "You're sort of like a Martian."

Each university has a slightly different policy on foreign teachers, but most follow the same general outline. As a holder of a B.A. or B.S. degree from an American college, you are qualified for the position of Foreign Teacher. A Masters Degree raises you to the designation of Foreign Expert. The key difference between the two positions, in most cases, is salary. As an instructor you will be paid, on the average, about 650 Yuan per month, or somewhere around $175 (in 1988, $1 = 3.7 Yuan). This is more than enough to support a comfortable lifestyle in China, and five or six times what beginning Chinese teachers earn.

Accommodations for foreign teachers are always separate from the regular dorms; the degree of isolation varies with the school. Some dormitories for foreign teachers are virtually next door to those of the Chinese students. Other foreign teachers are placed in guest houses off campus. The luxury spectrum is fairly broad, although even deluxe accommodations turn out to be pretty basic. "I know some people who had really nice three-room suites with kitchens," says Dan. "I had a small room and I had to beg for a year before I could get a small hotplate. But I was actually very happy with the living situation."

Whether or not you have cooking facilities makes an

enormous difference in your gastronomic life in China. With a kitchen, you can design your own Western diet using eggs, meat, and vegetables bought at the market. Coffee is rare, although you can get it at Friendship Stores and many tourist hotels. Likewise, milk and cheese and other dairy products don't play a big role in the Chinese diet. Beer, however, is good and plentiful. If you don't have the facilities to cook for yourself, the dormitory cafeteria or staff dining room will offer you traditional Chinese fare— noodles or rice for breakfast, and vegetables and meat (usually pork) over noodles or rice for lunch and dinner. "It helps to bring foods with you to China, like cheese, candy, and Lipton soups, anything that reminds you of home," says Stacy.

Your class schedule will be determined by the University. An optimum class load is 12 to 14 hours a week, although some former teachers have been saddled with twice that. "Some schools expect you to become an English teaching machine," says Russell. Subjects include basic English conversation and listening, English composition, and English reading comprehension. In general, English conversation and listening is easiest on the teacher, but unless the class is small, students often become lost and the teacher often becomes discouraged. "I know people who had 80 people in a conversation class," says Russell. "And there is no way you can teach." English composition means spending hours correcting papers, but many teachers find that their students are more candid about their lives and emotions on paper than in class discussions, so if you structure your assignments well, you can end up with quite an interesting education yourself. "I would give lectures and slide shows about issues in American culture, like housing in America, going out to eat in America," says Russell, "and then I would have them write essays on that issue in China. I would ask them to explain what their home was like, what their ideal home was like, and how they would deal with housing problems. It was a sneaky way to learn more, not just about practical aspects, but about what they were thinking."

Some universities have fixed lesson formats. Most, however, leave room for your own teaching style. "They gave us a book to use," says Dan, "but it was pretty bad and most of us tossed it." Chinese students are accustomed to learning by "filling the duck" or by rote, so encouraging student participation can be challenging. Most teachers rely heavily on role playing, skits, and games, although some of the older students lose patience with unorthodox methods. When all else fails, the topic of American culture usually livens things up. "All of my classes would end with a half hour discussion of American culture," says Stacy. "One day I gave a talk about disco music and I brought in clothes and makeup. I had a subscription to *Time* and *Mademoiselle,* which took care of current events and culture, and they loved that. If I go back there to teach this summer, I'll bring a sixty-minute tape of MTV."

Good textbooks are often in short supply in China, and former teachers and experts strongly recommend bringing books from home—elementary school readers, English as a second language (ESL) textbooks, magazines and novels. If you don't know exactly which courses you will be teaching, bring books that will cover all facets of English instruction. "It doesn't matter how heavy they are," says Stacy. "You will really need books."

You should expect to share your time outside of class with motivated students, earnest friendship seekers, and "English sharks," as overzealous students are sometimes called. Most teachers devote a few hours a week to formal tutoring or less structured conversation circles. "The classes were so big that I was thrilled if someone wanted to practice afterwards," says Dan. Stacy and her roommate held informal gatherings a few nights a week to which students were welcome to stop by for English and American

cookies. Some teachers, however, start to feel overwhelmed
by requests for extra-curricular English conversation or
special favors, like making purchases at the Friendship
Stores (which are open to foreigners only). There is a way
to prevent this predicament, however. "If you don't want to
get involved," says Russell, "just be polite and firm and tell
them you can't help them."

In addition to intellectual relationships, friendships between foreign teachers and Chinese students build quite
naturally and can be both emotionally satisfying and culturally helpful. "It's really important to find one close
Chinese friend to be a cultural bridge," says Russell. "That
person can help you understand problems. And if something goes wrong in the classroom, he or she can explain
why."

Extremely close friendships, though—including ro-
mances—can be messy, especially on the Chinese end.
Open-door policy aside, many of the traditional stigmas on
Western influences are still quite strong, especially outside
the big cities. And in pursuing or merely encouraging a
close relationship with one of your students, you might be
putting that person at risk. "One student was spending too
much time with us—he was with us all the time," says
Stacy—"and he was nearly expelled." At Stacy's school,
foreign teachers were monitored carefully, partly out of
concern for their own safety and partly, according to Stacy,
to see with whom they were spending time.

In considering a position teaching English in China, you
should also think about the realities of living in a country
so different from your own. Former students stress that for
all of China's natural and historical richness, it is very
much a Third World country. Many big cities are over-
crowded and filthy and people are quite poor. You will not
be insulated from these facts. "It's a very difficult life," says
Dan, "and you have to ask yourself how willing you are to
sacrifice material comforts." Teaching accommodations in

remote areas are often without heat and hot water, even during the frigid winters. "I'm a real California boy and I never got used to the cold," says Russell. "We would walk into our bathroom in the morning and the bottom of the shower floor would be frozen." Summers in many areas are scorching beyond the American imagination. Air conditioning is practically unheard–of outside Beijing and Shanghai, and even in those locations it's rare.

On a brighter note, parts of China are beautiful and exotic, and weekends and school vacations offer ample time to travel. Former teachers recommend steering clear of the tourist enclaves and big cities (with the exceptions of Shanghai and Canton) and venturing into the countryside and minority regions. Aside from Tibet, which is often closed off to foreigners, the area that seems to captivate young travelers most is the Southwest, an area that is rich in the culture of China's minority nationalities. The Yunnan Province, which borders Burma, Laos, and Vietnam is especially striking, offering gorges, lush jungles, mountain ranges, jagged cliffs, and villages that have changed little over thousands of years. Dali and Xishuangbanna are especially popular now, according to former teachers and travelers. And despite their charms and growing reputations, these areas are not yet overrun with tourists. Since most of China's ancient art and architecture was destroyed during the Cultural Revolution, these regions contain some of the last vestiges of traditional Chinese culture.

Traveling through China is extremely rewarding and affordable on a teachers' salary, but you must brace yourself for major run-ins with bureaucratic intransigence and overall inefficiency. Airplane rides can be harrowing (China Air has had a notoriously poor safety record), and long waits for train tickets often come up dry. ("I never waited in line at a train station for less than two hours," says Dan.) The same is true in many hotels. Your only recourse in these situations, former teachers agree, is good humor. "If a hotel clerk says they have no rooms, don't leave," says Russell. "Cajole the clerks. Smile, offer cigarettes, be persistent. After a while, you will win them over and usually they will end up helping you out. A lot of people get frustrated. But part of the fun is figuring out why it's happening. Keep an open mind and never lose sight of how ludicrous your situation is."

HOW TO GET A TEACHING POSITION IN CHINA

Teaching jobs in China are abundant, as any China-related organization or former teacher will tell you. Finding one, however, may take some patience. There are two ways to approach your search: through a placement program or by applying directly to individual universities.

PLACEMENT ORGANIZATIONS FOR RECENT GRADUATES

Of the handful of organizations that place teachers in Chinese universities, the following three offer the best prospects for recent graduates.

Princeton in Asia
222 Palmer Hall
Princeton, New Jersey 08544
(609) 452-3657

This program, the oldest and perhaps best known, places college graduates in teaching positions throughout Asia. You do not have to be a Princeton graduate to apply.

WorldTeach
Phillips Brooks House
Harvard University
Cambridge, Massachussetts 02138
(617) 495-5527

College graduates are eligible to teach English as a Second Language in China. As with WorldTeach's Kenya program, participants must subsidize their experience through the program fee, projected to be about $2,700. It includes airfare, room, and board. You do not have to be a Harvard graduate to qualify, although graduates who majored in arts and humanities are preferred over science majors.

University of Massachusetts Junior Teachers
   Program
Department of Asian Languages and Literatures
26 Thompson Hall
University of Massachusetts
Amherst, MA 01003
(413) 545-4350

Each year, this program sends a small number of recent graduates to teach at universities in China and Taiwan. Although they accept applications from graduates of any college, preference is given to UMASS graduates.

PROGRAMS FOR EXPERIENCED TEACHERS AND GRADUATE STUDENTS

China American Educational Exchange
College of Staten Island
715 Ocean Terrace, Room A323

Staten Island, New York 10301
(212) 988-7266

International Scientific & Information Services
49 Thompson Hay Path
Setauket, New York 11733
(516) 751-6437

US-China Peoples Friendship Association
18 Mansfield Place
Lynbrook, New York 11563
(516) 593-7225

The list of placement and exchange programs for qualified teachers changes constantly. For a free, annually updated list, contact the following organization:

National Committee on United States-China Relations
777 United Nations Plaza
New York, New York 10017-3521
(212) 922-1385

FINDING A POSITION ON YOUR OWN

If, for some reason, you do not find a position through a placement service, there is always the possibility of tracking one down by yourself. This is not a sure-fire route, and it requires an impressive amount of paper work, but most former teachers and program directors agree that if you are determined you will find a position. The names and addresses of about 150 Chinese universities follow. Experts agree that you should expect one job offer for every 20 letters sent out, so plan to send out at least 60 letters. (It's not as bad as it sounds—find a word processor and send out six letters a day for ten days.)

Don't send out these letters prior to the January or February preceding your graduation. The Chinese academic year begins in September and they don't get serious about foreign teaching placements until May, when budgets are set. If you send your letters too soon, they might get lost in the shuffle. Once you do send them, be patient. Some teachers have received acceptance letters as late as August. The Chinese, incidentally, do not customarily send out rejection letters, so you will likely hear only from schools that may have a position for you. One program director recommended including a simple self-addressed reply card to encourage the universities to notify you either way.

Your letter should be brief and very formal. State your interest in a foreign instructor position teaching English. Explain that you have a firm command of English grammar and form, and a clear, unaccented speaking voice. Outline your college academic record briefly, with special mention of English and Chinese courses. And most important, cite any and all experience you have that even remotely relates to teaching.

In addition to your letter, include a certified copy of your transcript and two or three letters of recommendation from professors, employers, counselors or other authority figures.

NEGOTIATING YOUR CONTRACT

As an independent teacher without the shelter of a placement program, it is extremely important that you work out the terms of your employment with the university, in writing, before you leave the United States. The following issues are top priority.

1. Your salary. As of fall, 1988, foreign instructors were receiving approximately 650 Yuan per month—about $175 according to 1988 exchange rates (salaries range from Y400 to Y800). Housing should be free, as should medical care. Some universities will pay your roundtrip air fare, although this privilege is usually reserved for foreign "experts."

2. Currency. In China, there are two types of currency: Renmibi (RMB) or "People's Money," which is what the Chinese people use, and Foreign Exchange Certificates (FEC), or "Tourist's Money," issued to people traveling through China. The key difference is that RMB cannot be exchanged for foreign currency and FEC can. Further, RMB is often not accepted in stores and hotels catering to foreigners. Many universities pay their foreign teachers' salaries in RMB only. Some teachers have been inconvenienced, especially when traveling, by their lack of FEC. So try to negotiate to receive a small part of your salary in FEC.

3. Your Teaching Schedule. Very important. A reasonable schedule includes about 12–14 hours of classes per week. 15 or 16 is still acceptable. More than 20 is not (unless you decide it is, once you get there).

● **CHINESE UNIVERSITIES**
(Direct all letters to the Foreign Affairs Office)

● **Anhui Normal University**
Wuhu City, Anhui

● **Anhui University**
Hefei, Anhui

- **Beijing Agricultural University**
  Beijing

- **Beijing College of Forestry**
  Beijing

- **Beijing College of Traditional Chinese**
  Medicine
  Beijing

- **Beijing Industrial University**
  Beijing

- **Beijing Institute of Aeronautics**
  Beijing

- **Beijing Institute of Agricultural**
  Mechanization
  Beijing

- **Beijing Institute of Chemical Technology**
  Beijing

- **Beijing Institute of Foreign Trade**
  Beijing

- **Beijing Institute of Foreign Languages**
  Beijing

- **Beijing Institute of Forestry**
  Beijing

- **Beijing Institute of Iron and Steel Technology**
  Beijing

- **Beijing Institute of Post and**
  Telecommunications
  Beijing

- **Beijing Institute of Technology**
  Beijing

- **Beijing Medical College**
  Beijing

- **Beijing Normal University**
  Beijing

- **Beijing Physical Culture Institute**
  Beijing

- **Beijing Teacher's College**
  Beijing

- **Beijing University**
  Beijing

- **Central China Agricultural Institute**
  Wuhan, Hubei

- **Central China Institute of Technology**
  Wuhan, Hubei

- **Central Institute of Fine Arts**
  Beijing

- **Central Music Conservatory**
  Beijing

- **Central South China Institute of Mining and Metallurgy**
  Changsha, Hunan

- **Changsha Engineering College**
  Changsha, Hunan

- **Changchun Institute of Geology**
  Changchun, Jilin

- **Chengdu Institute of Telecommunication Engineering**
  Chengdu, Sichuan

- **Chengdu University of Science and Technology**
  Chengdu, Sichuan

- **China Capital Medical University**
  Beijing

- **China Mining Institute**
  Xuzhou, Jiangsu

- **Chongqing Architectural Engineering Institute**
  Chongqing, Sichuan

- **Chongqing University**
  Chongqing, Sichuan

- **Dalian Institute of Technology**
  Dalian, Liaoning

- **Dalian Marine College**
  Dalian, Liaoning

- **Daqing Petroleum Institute**
  Daqing, Heilongjiang

- **East China Institute of Chemical Technology**
  Shanghai

- **East China Institute of Engineering**
  Nanjing, Jiangsu

- **East China Institute of Water Conservancy**
  Nanjing, Jiangsu

- **East China Petroleum Institute**
  Dongying, Shandong

- **East China Teacher's University**
  Shanghai

- **Fudan University**
  Shanghai

- **Fujian Normal University**
  Fuzhou, Fujian

- **Fuxin Mining Institute**
  Fuxin, Liaoning

- **Gansu Agricultural University**
  Wuwei, Gansu

- **Guangxi University**
  Nanning, Guangxi

- **Guizhou University**
  Guiyang, Guizhou

- **Hangzhou University**
  Hangzhou, Zhjiang

- **Harbin Institute of Technology**
  Harbin, Heilonjiang

- **Harbin Ship Engineering Institute**
  Harbin, Heilongjiang

- **Hebei Normal University**
  Shijiazhuang, Hebei

- **Hefei Polytechnical Institute**
  Hefei, Anhui

- **Heilongjiang University**
  Harbin, Heilongjiang

- **Henan University**
  Kaifeng, Henan

- **Huazhong Normal University**
  Wuhan, Hubei

- **Hunan Normal University**
  Changsha, Hunan

- **Hunan University**
  Changsha, Hunan

- **Inner Mongolia University**
  Hohhot, Inner Mongolia

- **International Relations Institute**
  Beijing

- **Jiangxi Agricultural University**
  Nanchang, Jiangxi

- **Jiangxi University**
  Nanchange, Jiangxi

- **Jilin Polytechnical University**
  Changchun, Jilin

- **Jilin University**
  Changchun, Jilin

- **Lanzhou University**
  Lanzhou, Gansu

- **Liaoning Normal University**
  Dalian, Liaoning

- **Nanjing Agricultural Institute**
  Nanjing, Jiangsu

- **Nanjing Institute of Aeronautics**
  Nanjing, Jiangsu

- **Nanjing Institute of Meteorology**
  Nanjing, Jiangsu

- **Nanjing Institute of Technology**
  Nanjing, Jiangsu

- **Nanjing Normal University**
  Nanjing, Jiangsu

- **Nanjing University**
  Nanjing, Jiangsu

- **Nankai University**
  Tianjin

- **North China Agricultural University**
  Zhengzhou, Henan

- **North China Institute of Electric Power**
  Baoding, Hebei

- **North China Jiaotong University**
  Beijing

- **Northeast China Heavy Machinery Institute**
  Fulaerji Heilongjiang

- **Northeast China Institute of Technology**
  Shenyang, Liaoning

- **Northeast Normal University**
  Jilin, Jilin

- **Northwest Agricultural Institute**
  Wugong, Shaanxi

- **Northwest China Institute of Light Industry**
  Xianyang, Shaanxi

- **Northwest China Institute of Technology**
  Xian, Shaanxi

- Northwest China Institute of Telecommunication Engineering
  Xian, Shaanxi

- Northwest China University
  Xian, Shaanxi

- Qinghua University
  Beijing

- Shaanxi Normal University
  Xian, Shaanxi

- Shandong College of Oceanography
  Qingdao, Shandong

- Shandong Normal University
  Jinan, Shandong

- Shandong University
  Jinan, Shandong

- Shanghai First Medical College
  Shanghai

- Shanghai Institute of Foreign Languages
  Shanghai

- Shanghai Jiaotong University
  Shanghai

- **Shanghai Teachers University**
  Shanghai

- **Shaanxi Agricultural Univeristy**
  Taigu, Shaanxi

- **Shengyang Agricultural University**
  Shengyang, Liaoning

- **Shenyang Teachers College**
  Shenyang, Liaoning

- **Sichuan Medical College**
  Chengdu, Sichuan

- **Sichuan Normal University**
  Chengdu, Sichuan

- **Sichuan University**
  Chengdu, Sichuan

- **South China Institute of Technology**
  Guangzhou, Guangdong

- **South China Normal University**
  Guangzhou, Guangdong

- **Southwest Agricultural Institute**
  Chongqing, Sichuan

- **Southwest China Jiaotong University**
  Emi County, Sichuan

- **Southwest Institute of Political Science & Law**
  Chongqing, Sichuan

- **Southwest Normal University**
  Chongqing, Sichuan

- **The Central Institute for Nationalities**
  Beijing

- **Tianjin Normal University**
  Tianjin

- **Tianjin University**
  Tianjin

- **Tianjin Foreign Languages Institute**
  Tianjin

- **Tongji University**
  Shanghai

- **University of International Business and**
  Economics
  Beijing

- **University of Science and Technology of**
  China
  Hefei, Anhui

- **Wuhan Geological Institute**
  Wuhan, Hubei

- **Wuhan Institute of Building Material Industry**
  Wuhan, Hubei

- **Wuhan Institute of Geodesy, Photogrammetry**
  & Cartography
  Wuhan, Hubei

- **Wuhan Institute of Water Conservancy &**
  Electric Power
  Wuhan, Hubei

- **Wuhan University**
  Wuhan, Hubei

- **Xiamen University**
  Xiamen, Fujian

- **Xian Jiaotong University**
  Xian, Shaanxi

- **Xiangtan University**
  Xiangtan, Hunan

- **Xinjiang University**
  Urumqi, Xinjiang

- **Yunnan University**
  Kunming, Yunnan

- **Zhejiang University**
  Hangzhou, Zhejiang

- **Zheijiang University**
  Hangzhou, Zhejiang

- **Zhenjiang Institute of Agricultural Machinery**
  Zhenjiang, Jiangsu

- **Zhongshan Medical College**
  Guangzhou, Guangdong

- **Zhongshan University**
  Guangzhou, Guandong

SUMMARY

Opportunities for Recent Graduates: Recent graduates are hired to teach English at Chinese universities.

Requirements: You must be a native speaker of English and hold a BA or BS from an American college. Some teaching experience is preferred.

Financial Arrangement: The current salary for college graduates is approximately 650 Yuan per month, or roughly $175, plus free housing. This is more than enough to live comfortably and travel through China, and five or six times what first-year Chinese teachers earn.

Time Frame: You must commit for at least one year, with the possibility of extending for a second year.

How to Apply: You can apply through a placement program or directly to the individual Chinese universities by sending the following:

- A letter of inquiry

- Certified copies of your transcript

- Two or three letters of recommendation

- Self-addressed reply cards (to encourage responses)

Pros:

- Unique experience in cultural immersion.

- Engaging people.

- Fascinating travel opportunities.

Cons:

- Frustrating bureaucracy.

- Harsh physical conditions.

- Possibly difficult application process.

Travel Opportunities: Travel is cheap and rewarding, but often difficult due to bureaucratic entanglements, crowded conditions, and general inefficiency. Patience is required. Former teachers recommend making an effort to see minority areas such as Tibet, Lijiang, Xishuangbanna, and Dali.

RECOMMENDED READING

China: A Travel Survival Kit, by Alan Samagalski, Michael Buckley, and Robert Strauss. Lonely Planet's widely recommended budget travel book, packed with tips on what to see, where to stay, and what to eat ($14.95, Lonely Planet Publications, 112 Linden Street, Oakland, California 94607; (415) 893-8555).

China Bound, by Karen Turner-Gottschang and Linda A. Reed. This book, compiled by the Committee on Scholarly Communication with the People's Republic of China, is a guide for teachers working in China ($14.95, National Academy Press, 2101 Constitution Avenue, N.W., Washington, D.C. 20418 (202) 334-3313).

Iron and Silk, by Mark Salzman. This wonderful book chronicles Salzman's experiences and adventures working as an English teacher at the Hunan Medical College from 1982 to 1984 ($5.95, Vintage Departures/Random House, widely available at bookstores).

Southwest China: Off the Beaten Track, by K. Mark Stevens and George E. Wehrfritz. Based on the 16-month odyssey of two young travelers, this book is the only book you need to explore China's most beautiful region ($12.95, Passport Books, in conjunction with the Guidebook Company Limited).

NOTE: If you can't find these books in a local bookstore, you can order them from China Books:

136 West 18th Street
New York, New York 10011
(212) 627-4044

2929 24th Street
San Francisco, California 94110
(415) 282-2994

GUATEMALA

Peace Brigades International
International Office
4722 Baltimore Avenue
Philadelphia, Pennsylvania 19143
(215) 724-1464

Central American Projects Office
175 Carlton Street
Toronto, Canada M5A 2K3
(416) 595-9484

Through their quiet presence, Karen, Elizabeth, Ken, and other volunteers from Peace Brigades International (PBI) promote non-violence in Guatemala and El Salvador. They come to these countries, where death threats and "disappearances" are a fact of life, and work as low-profile escorts to human rights activists, labor leaders, and other people whose efforts to bring about peace make them prime targets for violence. They don't carry weapons, but they are armed with access to a vast international community that would broadcast news of a shooting or kidnapping around the world. And since the tormentors in these countries are image conscious, PCB volunteers have, in many cases, been able to prevent violence. "Our presence raises the political price of violence," says Chip, a former volunteer and current PBI staff member. "The volunteers are backed by an international political organization that would respond immediately if something were to happen to the people they are escorting."

In the case of Grupo De Apoyo Mutuo (GAM), a human rights organization that aids the families of Guatemala's disappeared, PCB's effectiveness is especially apparent. Before PCB got involved, the group was plagued by violence. Two of its leaders were killed, and death threats to other members were commonplace. Since 1985, though, when PCB began escorting its leaders and attending its meetings, GAM has been free of violence. It is the first human rights organization to survive in recent history, and plays a significant role in fighting for human rights throughout Guatemala.

If this sounds like serious business, it is. PCB volunteers spend most of their time in those places most likely to attract violence—strikes, demonstrations, meetings of human rights leaders. At the same time, since it was founded in 1981, no volunteer has ever been harmed. And though fear is something all PCB volunteers must confront, they maintain that it does not characterize the experience.

"Being a volunteer gives you a chance to visit a country and experience the reality of it," says Ken, a recent volunteer. "It's stepping beyond tourism. You get a truer portrait of what life is like in this country. And while you're learning, you're able to do something about it."

Volunteers can serve for as little as two months or as long as two years. Recent graduates without any direct ex-

perience will likely be placed in Guatemala, where PCB is
recognized by the goverment (the situation is more complex
in El Salvador). In Guatemala, a communal house just outside Guatemala City is the base of PCB's operations. Volunteers work five days each week, for twenty-four hours at
a stretch. The most common task is escorting, which means
accompanying someone throughout their daily activities
and usually spending the night at their house. "The main
thing is to be as unobtrusive as possible," says Ken. "For
instance if the person you're escorting meets someone for
dinner, you would sit at a different table so that you could
keep them in sight but give them space." Another typical
volunteer activity is escorting groups, such as strikers,
demonstrators, and marchers. "You don't demonstrate or
march yourself," says Ken. "You just observe."

For the most part, volunteers see little in the way of
violence. And many serve for a year without seeing so much
as a wrongful glance. But they are trained to notice warn-
ing signs. "There were times when I would notice something the average person wouldn't notice," says Ken. "Like
I'd be walking down the street and a block behind there's a
car with tinted windows idling up the street." In the event
something does happen, they are to document it (volunteers
carry cameras) and start the notification process as soon as
possible. They do not function as bodyguards.

The pressures of this volunteer position should not be
minimized. But, volunteers were quick to explain, neither
should the rewards and the benefits. One of the greatest
benefits to volunteers, particularly those in Guatemala, is
the chance to get to know a country that is endlessly interesting and beautiful. Volunteers often spend days off traveling, to the Mayan ruins in Guatemala's Tikal and Petan
and to Indian villages like Chichicastenagno and Panajachel, to the seashores and the lakes. "We see all of the
wonderful things to see in Guatemala," says Ken. "There's
plenty of time to do that."

PCB looks for volunteers who have a deep commitment to nonviolence, who have "an openness to cultural understanding," as Karen puts it, and the maturity to adapt to an internationl living experience. There are no particular prerequisites, except a solid command of Spanish. "People must be able to understand what's happening in an emergency situation," says Maya, a PCB staff member.

There are currently about 20 volunteers in the field. And while PCB is always looking for volunteers, their applications are increasing.

SUMMARY

Who They Are: Peace Brigades International, a non-partisan organization, provides escort protection and an international presence for people and groups committed to nonviolence.

Where: Guatemala and El Salvador.

Opportunities For Recent Graduates: Volunteers escort human rights activists and labor leaders and other individuals and groups threatened with violence. They also serve as a witness for the international community.

Financial Arrangements: Volunteers must pay their own way down to Central America. PCI provides room and board and a small stipend.

Time Frame: From two months to two years.

Number of Positions: Approximately twenty.

How to Apply: The staff of the Philadelphia office is available to answer questions. But the most direct way to apply is to contact the Toronto office directly.

Pros:

- Learning about complex political situation.

- Promoting non violence.

- Fascinating travel opportunities.

Cons:

- Undercurrent of danger.

Travel Opportunities: Guatemala is a beautiful country with a strong indigenous Indian culture. It's also quite small, so even remote areas are accessible within a few hours by bus or plane. Among the numerous areas of interest are the hundreds of Mayan ruins in Tikal and The Petan, the village of Panajachel on the shores of Lake Attilan, and the Indian village of Chichicastenango.

ISRAEL

The following two opportunities—working on a kibbutz and the Sherut La'am volunteer program—are available in Israel. Though Israel is a Jewish nation, you do not have to be Jewish to participate in either of these two opportunities, or, for that matter, to appreciate Israel's beauty, history, and spirit.

Israel, as anyone who has been there will tell you, is a gorgeous country. And it is so small that you can travel from north to south in a six-hour bus ride, making day and weekend trips pleasant and easy. Its natural landscape—the serene Mediterranean beaches, imposing mountain ranges, and desert oases—are striking at any time of year, but especially in the spring, when even the deserts seem to bloom. Add to that hundreds of archaeological sites that reflect thousands of years of history—like Caesarea, near Tel Aviv—a most impressive site that includes a well-preserved Roman amphitheater and bath, Byzantine streets, and an elaborate Crusader city.

Underscoring Israel's natural serenity, however, is the palpable tension of a country which has fought tenaciously for survival. You should be prepared for tight security and the sight of many citizens with automatic weapons slung casually over their shoulders. None of the recent graduates I spoke to, however, felt at risk, or that the tension detracted from their experience. It's simply a fact of life. "There's something extremely moving about Israel, the whole notion of a cause, of a common human endeavor," says Suzy, a former Sherut La'am volunteer. "I don't think you have to be Jewish to feel it. I'm not Jewish, and I felt it strongly. I just think you have to be human."

> **Sherut La'am**
> American Zionist Youth Foundation
> 515 Park Avenue
> New York, New York 10022
> (212) 751-6070

Sherut La'am is primarily a volunteer placement service. Its name means "service to the people." But while most participants end up working in areas populated by Israel's more disadvantaged ethnic minorities, other participants have taken advantage of the program's flexibility and shaped an experience that is more like a work-abroad program than a volunteer program. Whatever your motivations, Sherut La'am is a great way to live and work in Israel. It provides you with a foundation of Hebrew, an interesting job—often in a field that relates to your career interests—and a monthly stipend to cover your living expenses.

Sherut La'am's mandate is to find college graduates to fill human service jobs in communities known as "development towns." These towns, planned communities built in the past 40 years, house many of the thousands of immigrants who have fled to Israel—Holocaust survivors, Yememites, Ethiopians, Moroccans, Russians, Romanians and others. The towns are designed to offer a cheap, comfortable haven and a sense of community to people who arrive in Israel with little money and no job prospects. Many end up setting down permanent roots. The few dozen development towns scattered throughout Israel range in population from about 5,000 to 20,000. Each one has a different flavor, but they are generally poor, extremely cohesive, and potently ethnic. Crime is practically non-existent, family bonds are strong, and volunteers are warmly welcomed.

Before you settle into a development town, you will spend three months with other Sherut La'am volunteers learning Hebrew in an ulpan (intensive Hebrew course) on a college campus, a kibbutz, or immigration center. Hebrew is not a complicated language, despite its daunting alphabet. And many people emerge from their ulpan nearly fluent. "How much you learn depends on how much you work," says Suzy, a Sherut La'am volunteer. "There were some people who carried index cards around wherever they went, and they came out really knowing the language."

At some point during the ulpan, you will be asked to select a development town where you will spend the balance of your service. To help you make your decision, representatives from different development towns converge on the ulpan site to tell you about job opportunities and to paint a picture of life in their towns. If you can't make up your mind, Sherut La'am will pay for visits to a few towns until you find one you like. Your decision could relate to your job preferences (employment opportunities vary from town to town) geographical preferences (you might want to be near a large city or close to a beach), or plain instinct. "I liked the fact that there were flowers all over and that I could walk everywhere," says Carol, who served in the town of Kiriyat-Gat. "Also, there were a few other volunteers serving there, but not tons."

Sherut La'am pays for your housing, usually a small apartment you share with another volunteer or two. "We had one of the nicest apartments," says Carol. "We had a television to share with another apartment, and a telephone, which is pretty uncommon." Since most of the organizations employing Sherut La'am volunteers can't afford to pay salaries, Sherut La'am provides you with a stipend of $180 per month for food and expenses, which volunteers say is just about enough. You should bring along some money of your own for traveling.

Your job, in most cases, will involve substantial responsibility, even if you don't have any specific experience. Most volunteers return to the United States with some serious job experience racked up. Past participants have worked as law assistants, medical assistants, English teachers, counselors, and environmental planners. Carol, for one, spent her mornings teaching English and her afternoons working with children and adolescents from troubled homes. "You can do almost any sort of work, even if you've never done anything like it before." says Carol. "It's great because you can really see what the profession is like. I know people who helped in hospitals and hadn't studied anything medical before." Adds Andrew, another Sherut La'am volunteer: "You can live out your fantasies."

The social life in Israel revolves around the home. "In New York, if you want to see someone, you call them and ask them if you can come over," says Suzy. "In Israel, you just drop by. It's very social. People always have cakes around because they never know when company will come around." Your liaison to your community is an "adoptive family" assigned to you at the beginning of your term. "I was always welcome at my family's home," says Carol, whose adoptive family was a Moroccan couple and their four grown children. "I would eat dinner with them regularly, and see them a few times a week. They introduced me to their friends and family and I became friends with some of their kids, who were in the army and would come home on weekends." Some development towns are located in remote parts of Israel. But because the country is so small, you are never more than an hour or two away from a city or a fellow Sherut La'am volunteer.

Still, some Sherut La'am volunteers want to live in a big city, most often in Jerusalem. The organization's staff members don't encourage this, but they usually support the decision. "They want this to be a good experience for you," says Andrew. "They want you to be happy, to show you that you can do the same things in Israel that you can do in the United States. The idea is that if you have a good experience, you will think about moving here permanently, although they don't pressure you at all." Adds Suzy: "They gave me a hard time at first. Then they said that if I could find a job, I could stay. They were lovely about it. I got a great job and I had an incredible experience."

One of the drawbacks of working in Jerusalem is that Sherut La'am volunteers don't receive the same structure and guidance given those serving in development towns. It's up to you to find a place to live, which can be difficult, considering Jerusalem's housing shortage. Some volunteers find apartments through friends, as Thea, Andrew, and Libby did. Suzy went through an apartment-finding service, which charged a small fee. You will also have to pay for your housing, which will cost approximately $150 a month for a modest, shared apartment in a good section of town. "I lived with four people in a beautiful four-bedroom apartment in Germantown, which is one of the nicest neighborhoods," says Thea. "We pooled our expenses and I wound up paying $250 a month for rent, food and utilities." Volunteers who choose to serve in Jerusalem receive a slightly higher stipend, but to make ends meet you may still have to dip into personal savings ($100 to $150 a month should be enough), or find a part-time job, like cleaning houses. (It's not bad—the jobs are easy to get and lots of people do it," says Thea.)

The job options in Jerusalem are vast, but they're not as neatly laid out as they are in the development towns, and you'll have to approach the search as seriously as you would in a major American city. Despite this, however, past participants have been extremely successful. Andrew, utterly resolved to land a job in communications, wound up as an English-language reporter for Israel Radio. He traveled throughout the country, interviewed Israel's president Shamir, received personal tours of newly opened archaeological sites, and had his stories aired all over the world. "I was a person with no professional experience and they let me do any kind of stories I wanted." Thea worked for a civil rights organization, a "dream job," in her words. Libby worked at a school for children with cerebral palsy. In all of these cases, the Sherut La'am staff helped by providing contacts and suggestions. "I went to them and said, 'One of you must know someone at Israel Radio,' " says Andrew. "And sure enough, someone did."

Living and working in a major city has its obvious benefits. Jerusalem is an especially pretty city with a cosmopolitan population. Despite its being small and relatively conservative, it has, as one Sherut La'am volunteer put it, "a nervous energy." The development towns can't compete with the cities in terms of diversions, but development towns do have a strong element of community that Sherut La'am volunteers can share. You won't find this sense of community in Jerusalem, where meeting Israelis is difficult and many Sherut La'am volunteers revert to socializing with a large population of Americans. "There are lots of English speakers in Jerusalem and you have to be very demanding to practice your Hebrew," says Libby. Adds Suzy, "I would have made more Israeli friends if I had served in a development town."

Sherut La'am offers two types of programs—the one–year program with an ulpan and a six-month program for people who already know Hebrew. Both programs are open to college graduates, ages 20 to 35.

SUMMARY

Who They Are: Sherut La'am, a program sponsored by the World Zionist Organization, places college graduates in volunteer jobs in Israel.

Opportunities for Recent Graduates: Recent graduates can live and work in ethnic development towns— planned communities built in the past 40 years to house many of the thousands of immigrants who have fled to Israel. Occasionally, Sherut La'am volunteers serve in Jerusalem and other cities.

Financial Arrangement: If you serve in a development town, Sherut La'am will pay for your housing and provide a monthly stipend of $180 per month to cover food and expenses. If you serve in Jerusalem, you must pay for your housing, but you will receive a slightly inflated stipend. Each participant must pay a preliminary program fee of $300 plus a $50 application fee. You must also pay for your airfare, which costs about $1,000.

Time Frame: There are two Sherut La'am programs. The one–year program includes an initial three–month ulpan, or intensive Hebrew course, plus nine months of working. The six–month program, for people who already know Hebrew, will place you directly in your work situation.

Number of Volunteers: There are approximately 25 people in each volunteer group.

Pros:

- Serious work experience.

- A flexible program.

- Community kinship in development towns.

Cons:

- A six-day work week.

- Lack of diversions in development towns.

- A relatively high American population in Jerusalem.

Living on a Kibbutz
Kibbutz Aliyah Desk
27 West 20th Street, 9th Floor
New York, New York 10011
(212) 255-1338

As a kibbutz volunteer, you enter into a uniquely Israeli institution, a style of life that has weathered conflict and change since the first kibbutz came together in 1909, but yet has remained remarkably true to its founding ideal—that people can live and work together as equals.

A kibbutz is a community in which everything is owned and administered collectively by the kibbutz members, or "kibbutzniks." They support themselves through farming and manufacturing, and they use volunteers to bolster their productivity and to fill in for kibbutzniks serving in the army. Although you must be Jewish to become a full-fledged kibbutznik, you don't have to be Jewish to be a volunteer. And indeed, a large portion are not. "Out of about 50 volunteers, I was the only Jewish person," says Lynn, who spent time on a kibbutz between her freshman and sophomore year.

There are more than 250 kibbutzim scattered throughout Israel today. The largest kibbutz has close to 2,000 members; the smallest has four. Most, with between 250 and 500 members, are like small towns, vibrant and eclectic, complete with farms and factories, schools, libraries, swimming pools, stores, dance clubs, and sports teams. Members live in well-appointed apartments, equipped with their own furniture, stereos, television and other personal items.

As a kibbutz volunteer, you will receive free room, three meals a day, some pocket change, and full use of the kibbutz resources. In exchange, you will work. Hard. For 40

hours a week, six to eight hours a day, volunteers work in
the fields and factories, in the dining rooms, kindergartens,
chicken coops, laundry rooms, and kitchens. You might be
roused at four A.M. to pick avocados or assigned to the midnight factory shift putting together lawn chairs on an assembly line. "The work is definitely hard, and pretty
boring," says Lynn. "There I was, in this huge field of
grapes with eight other people and about 20 jugs of water.
It's so hot you have to drink constantly. And my job was to
walk up and down the field, cleaning tiny leaves off the
grapevines. You work from about five to seven-thirty in the
morning, when you break for water and oranges. Then you
go back to work until nine o'clock, when you break for
breakfast. The work really isn't bad. There was a radio
going, and we were singing to make the time go by. And
there's a feeling of accomplishment when you finish a field.
I got a real sense of myself through the physical labor."

While equality is a much-touted maxim on kibbutzim,
kibbutzniks are not immune from Israel's pervasive male
chauvinism. And job assignments for both members and
volunteers are subject to sexist stereotypes. In the work
force, it's rare to see a woman performing strenuous labor
in the factories or fields, and even rarer to see a man cooking, sewing or caring for children. The same goes for volunteers. And although the kibbutznik in charge of
volunteer job assignments is receptive to job requests, you
are at the mercy of the needs of the kibbutz. New volunteers are generally placed in the most menial positions—
on the assembly lines, in the orchards, at the kitchen sink,
or in the day-care center. "There's a hierarchy of jobs
among volunteers," says Thea. "The longer you stay, the
more chance you have for upward mobility. But it's all relative. If you stay for three months on an assembly line, you
might be upgraded to a fork lift, which will seem very exciting."

Work is indeed taken seriously on kibbutzim. And even

those with slothful tendencies tend to rise to the ethic. But as any volunteer will tell you, there is more to life on kibbutzim than working. The work day, for one thing, is usually over by noon or so. And once you put in your six to eight hours, you are totally free to explore, to read and relax by yourself, and to get to know your fellow volunteers, who will likely represent countries from all over the world. "We had people from England, France, South America, Canada, Japan, Germany . . . " says Thea, who has spent several stints as a kibbutz volunteer. "It was a very interesting group."

Furthermore, the benefits you receive in exchange for your toil are generous. Virtually all of your material needs are taken care of, often with considerable panache. You will live in a dorm situation with the other volunteers. Since the fields and factories are tough on clothes, the kibbutz will provide you with work attire. It will also do your laundry for you. "You just attach a name tag to whatever you need washed, and a few days later it comes back to you," says Lynn. Meals are bountiful and delicious feasts— fresh vegetables, home-baked breads and cakes, fresh cheese, milk, and yogurt, meats, fruits—certainly enough to cover most of your cravings. "Everyone gains weight on kibbutzim, no matter how hard the work," says Lisa.

Soap, shampoo, cleaning materials, pens, aerograms, and other incidentals are available for the asking. "Everything is there," says Lynn. "And you just take as much as you need." Many kibbutzim also provide you with a small amount of cash each week, maybe five or ten dollars, which you can use at the kibbutz bar (liquor isn't free) or apply to your travels.

The kibbutz volunteer coordinator will usually structure some activities for the volunteers—weekend camping trips at the beach, hikes in the mountains, excursions into towns. In the evenings there are often movies, dances, and parties. But since the volunteer community is usually young and fairly sizable—sometimes more than a hundred people—the atmosphere is naturally quite social. The specifics of the social life seem to vary from kibbutz to kibbutz, depending on the size and the makeup of the volunteer community. Some volunteers describe a scene that is reminiscent of summer camp, with volunteers relaxing together outside, talking, playing guitars, and cutting each other's hair. Other volunteers say the atmosphere is more like a fraternity party, with plenty of drinking, romance, and late nights (most kibbutzim provide alarm clocks for early morning shifts).

There is, for the most part, little close interaction between volunteers and kibbutzniks. Although meals and work are shared, the two communities exist quite separately, and most volunteers agree that the general attitude of kibbutzniks toward volunteers is, at best, standoffish. "The first night I sat down for dinner and didn't understand why no one at the table was talking to me," says Lynn. "Then I realized that I had sat at a table of kibbutzniks. The next night I sat with volunteers."

This unfriendliness, long-term volunteers agree, is not to be taken personally. "It's hard for them to make friends with people and have them constantly leave," says Thea. And some volunteers claim that the longer you serve as a volunteer, the more you are able to penetrate the exterior of coldness. "My best friends in Israel are kibbutzniks," says Thea. "I returned there after a year and a half, and the bond had strengthened. They're just like my siblings. And their homes are my homes."

Still, most volunteers remain within the boundries of the volunteer community. And some, looking for more cultural intensity than the volunteer community can generate, come away disappointed. "I came here wanting to learn about Israel," says Lisa. "The kibbutzniks weren't eager to make friends, and I ended up with a group of volunteers I didn't have much in common with."

If you don't find exactly what you are looking for on the kibbutz itself, you might pursue an interest outside the gates. A typical kibbutz will allow one day off for every six days worked, in addition to the traditional Saturday day of rest. You can take these days off as they come up, or let them accrue into longer vacations.

Since most kibbutzim have an ongoing need for volunteers, finding a position is easy. You can't, however, simply arrive at a kibbutz and expect to be taken in. You must apply in advance, through one of the many kibbutz representatives around the world. It generally takes about six weeks for your application to be processed. There are more than a dozen representative organizations in the United States, the largest being New York's Kibbutz Alliya Desk. In addition to handling your application and arranging for a personal interview, a kibbutz representative will help you find a kibbutz that suits you in terms of size, location, and language. (Hebrew is the main language on most kibbutzim, but English, German, French, and Spanish are commonly used.) Also, if you are interested in learning Hebrew, you can request a kibbutz with an ulpan, or intensive Hebrew program.

SUMMARY

What It Is: A kibbutz is a community in which everything is owned and administered collectively by its members, the "kibbutzniks." Most kibbutzim, with between 250 to 500 members, are like small towns, complete with their own schools, libraries and commerce.

Where: There are more than 250 kibbutzim in virtually every area of Israel.

Opportunities For Recent Graduates: Kibbutzim day-care centers, kitchens, and nearly all other areas of the kibbutz.

Financial Arrangement: You will work approximately forty hours a week (spread over six days). In exchange, you will receive free room (a dormitory-style room, usually shared with one or two other volunteers), three meals a day (generally of very high quality), toiletries, housekeeping supplies, laundry service, a small amount of pocket money, and full use of the kibbutz facilities.

Time Frame: Most kibbutzim invite volunteers to stay for one month to one year. (A few will let you stay longer.)

Number of Volunteers: Depending on the size and age of the kibbutz, the volunteer community might number more than a hundred people, mostly young, from all over the world.

How to Apply: You must apply in advance, as most kibbutzim will not accept walk-ins. One of the dozen kibbutz representatives in the United States will process your application, interview you, and find you a place that suits your interests and needs. Contact the Kibbutz Alliya Desk for more information.

Pros:

- Unique, altenative lifestyle.

- Volunteers from all over the world.

- Generous benefits.

Cons:

- Aloof kibbutzniks.

- Strenuous, tedious work.

- An inflexible work routine.

Travel Opportunities: Most kibbutzim offer one day off for every six days of work, plus a traditional day of rest on Saturday. You can take the days off as they come up, or let them accrue for a longer period.

JAPAN

TEACHING ENGLISH IN JAPAN

Teaching English in Japan has supplanted the Eurail trip through Europe as the odyssey of popular choice among many recent graduates and serious young travelers. Indeed, it has achieved near cliché status, inspiring a book, *Ransom,* by Jay McInerney, and a predictable backlash of rumors about prohibitively high prices, throngs of ugly Americans, and xenophobia among the Japanese.

There is some truth to these rumors and in aspects of McInerney's rather empty depiction of the American teacher life-style. But there is another side to the story, one involving endless job options, huge salaries, and an intriguing culture. And this is the image that has lured tens of thousands of native English speakers to Japan in the past decade.

Most English-teacher candidates head to Japan blindly, with no job prospects and no contacts, and this proves to be a course that generally works surprisingly well. "I went over there, I didn't have a job, I didn't know the language, and I didn't know anyone," says Victoria, a Harvard graduate who spent nine months as a teacher in Kyoto. "But I knew I could get a job teaching English, and I did."

Nonetheless, there are some things you should know about the world into which you are delving, and there are some factors to consider before setting out, the most important being your finances. Since the value of the yen has surged in the past few years—from about 220 yen to the dollar in 1985 to 132 yen to the dollar in late 1988—today's hopeful teachers must arrive in Japan with roughly twice the amount of money as those arriving in 1985. The cost of living in Japan, as you undoubtedly know, is extremely high. And veteran English teachers agree that you should arrive in Japan with no less than $2,500 seed money to support yourself while you are looking for a job and subsequently waiting for your first paycheck to be processed. (This can take up to one month from your first day of work.)

Second, you should realize that while the independent teacher route is the most popular choice among young people, it is not your only option. There is a program called the Japanese Exchange and Teaching Program (JET), administered through the Japanese embassy in Washington, which recruits college graduates from America, Great Britain, and Australia to be assistant English teachers in Japanese high schools. More than 600 Americans participated in JET in 1988, and more than 900 are slated for 1989.

The main advantages of the JET program are that you can set up a job before you leave the states, and you are guaranteed a yearly salary of 3,200,000 yen (roughly $27,000, according to late 1988 exchange rates). This is more than twice what first-year Japanese teachers earn, and will support a pleasant life-style in Japan. In addition, your employer will buy you a round trip plane ticket to Japan.

But there are some drawbacks as well. As a JET recruit,

you are bound to an 11-month contract (from August to July) and a 40-hour week, which is twice that of the average independent teacher. And you have little control over where in Japan you are placed. The schools are located in all types of communities—cities, suburbs, towns, and rural villages.

Overall, the JET program is best suited for someone whose prevailing goal for their year off is to learn about Japanese culture. You will sacrifice some freedom, but in exchange, you will experience a side of Japan that few independent teachers ever see. (For complete information, contact: **Japanese Exchange and Teaching Program, Embassy of Japan, 2520 Massachusetts Avenue, N.W., Washington, D.C. 20008, (202) 939-6700.**)

The independent-teacher route gives you more control over your life-style. You make your own hours, select your jobs, decide how hard you want to work and how much money you want to earn. Though you must make all of your own arrangements, the path is well marked, so you should run into little trouble along the way.

Your first decision as an independent teacher is where in Japan you want to settle. Although the demand for English teachers is high throughout Japan, the prime locations are Tokyo and Kyoto—Tokyo for its unsurpassed job opportunities and Kyoto for its scenery and rich culture. "Kyoto is generally compared to Boston," says Chris, a UCLA graduate who split a year and a half between both places. "It's pretty, historic, and a manageable place to live. Tokyo is like New York—exciting and energetic. There are lots of jobs to choose from and different kinds of people. But it is crowded, dirty, and not very attractive."

Both cities are brimming with teaching opportunities, especially in private language schools. And even if you have no previous experience, finding a job is fairly easy (although it might take a bit longer in Kyoto). Still, plan to approach your job search seriously, dressed professionally and armed with multiple copies of your college diploma or transcript, plus a couple of letters of recommendation from teachers or employers. Give yourself a few days to survey the job market and don't commit to a particular school until you are convinced it's the best opportunity for you. "Take your time," says Chris. "Talk to other foreigners, visit the schools, compare salaries and hours, and then make up your mind."

The salaries and conditions in private language schools vary dramatically, from top-notch establishments that pay teachers 4,000 to 5,000 yen per hour (about $30 an hour on the low end, according to late 1988 exchange rates), to low-rent institutions offering as little as 1,500 yen (about $11). As of late 1988, the average salaries at the respectable schools were somewhere just above 3,000 yen per hour, or about $24. If you have taught before or have taken any education courses (particularly in English as a second language), you will be eligible for a higher salary. Be sure to bring appropriate documentation.

A typical class load falls between 12 and 20 hours per week; prime teaching hours are between 5:00 and 9:00 P.M. to accommodate business executives. Morning and afternoon classes are less common, but most schools offer a few, catering mainly to housewives. "They squeeze in English classes between their cooking classes, flower arranging classes, and aerobics," says Victoria.

The classes, for the most part, are intended to offer a comfortable, low-pressure environment for students to practice speaking English. Most of your students will have already had many years of formal English instruction, but while they can ace tests on grammar and usage, few can hold up their end of an intelligible conversation. "The stereotype of a Japanese English student is one who is shy and nervous," says Chris. "This is not true of everyone, but in general, it is pretty accurate. At first, it is challenging to get them to open their mouths—they are reluctant to make mistakes, and embarrassed unless they have it down perfectly. But with time, they become more comfortable, and your job gets easier."

Although some people have secured jobs with private language schools before leaving the United States, veteran teachers strongly recommend waiting until you get to Japan. If, however, you want to start investigating your options before you leave, I strongly recommend John Wharton's wonderful book, *Jobs in Japan*. Names and addresses of more than two-hundred schools in Japan are listed, and the author offers good-humored advice about taking on the job market and adjusting to life in Japan.

Once you arrive in Japan, there are several helpful resources available to help you with your job search. A number of English language newspapers list advertisements for English teachers in their classified sections. You'll find the most listings in the Japan *Times* and the Tokyo *Journal* for the Tokyo area, while the Mainichi *Daily News* and Kansai *Time Out* target the Kyoto area. In addition, many of the hotels, clubs, and restaurants frequented by foreigners have job bulletin boards. The bulletin board at the Kimi Information Center, attached to the Kimi Ryokan (an inn frequented by foreign visitors) is especially active.

But your best source of information about job opportunities, veterans agree, is other English teachers and expatriates. The tight network of foreign teachers in both Tokyo and Kyoto circulates news on teaching positions, apartment vacancies, and other important information. "The best way to find out about jobs is by word of mouth," says Victoria. "There are always people leaving jobs."

The quickest way to tap into this network is by spending some time at one of the small minshiku (pensions), dormitories, or ryokans (Japanese-style guest houses), which are frequented by foreigners. In addition to providing a cheap, clean, and comfortable place to stay (anywhere from $9 to

$40 per night) while you familiarize yourself with the city,
these places are ideal repositories of information. "The first
place I stayed at was a small boardinghouse where you get
a small room and share a bathroom and central kitchen,"
says Victoria. "These places are usually convenient, Americans are there, and the management speaks English. This
was a nice place because I learned about jobs, housing,
roommates, friends. And you meet people who speak your
language to ask about job interviews and to go have a beer.
There's a bonding that goes on."

A list of those hotels and inns most often mentioned by
veteran teachers and guide books can be found on page 73.
The Tourist Information Centers (TIC) at Tokyo's Narita
airport and downtown Tokyo and Kyoto also make available up-to-date lists of moderately priced accommodations.

Your fellow foreigners can introduce you to the lucrative
teaching jobs available outside of private language schools
—jobs with families, corporations, businesses, and individuals that can pay two and three times the language school
salary. "Just about the time I was leaving, I was recommended for a job at a sports complex that paid $70 per hour,
six hours a day," says Victoria. Jobs like these filter
through the foreigner network, but they are usually
snapped up quickly. So you should seek leads on your own.
Many English teachers have found private clients by post-
ing notices throughout the city—in bars, on tourist office
bulletin boards, in restaurants. This device works best if
you can show credentials that an average Japanese person
might identify with—say, a degree from a top college, or
work experience with a Japanese or high-profile international company. Japanese contacts, people who can introduce you around and vouch for your character, are perhaps
the best source of such jobs. "The Japanese run according
to trust," says Victoria.

Teaching English is the bread and butter for most young
foreigners working in Japan. But there are some other op-

tions, particularly if you have imagination. Modeling is the most common alternative to teaching, and if you have confidence in your physical endowments, you should certainly give it a shot. In addition to the more traditional types of fashion modeling and commercial work, where the standards are not much lower than they are in this country, many Japanese businesses use attractive foreigners to adorn their clothing stores, eyeglass stores, restaurants, and bars. The work isn't terribly stimulating, but the pay is generally quite good. The best way to find out about these jobs is through the classified ads of the newspapers and magazines mentioned earlier.

And if you have a particular talent or skill—cooking, sewing, dancing, tennis—try to market it. "The sky is the limit if you are creative," says Victoria. "You have to be tuned in to the culture to know what they want. If you know how to cook, for example, you could teach simple French cooking to the Japanese. The Japanese are very receptive to the idea of classes."

How hard you work in Japan is up to you. Figure that you will need to earn at least 250,000 yen ($2,000) per month to live well and to afford to travel. An above-average teaching job and perhaps one sideline, such as a private tutoring arrangement, should cover this easily. Rent will cost anywhere between 40,000 yen and 100,000 yen per month ($300 to $750), depending on whether you live in a dormitory, a guest house, or an apartment. If you have your heart set on an apartment, be prepared to hand over as much as six months' rent up front as a deposit to your landlord (and figure such funds into the amount of money you bring from home).

Veterans agree that a key to keeping expenses under control is learning to live Japanese–style. American restaurants are expensive, as are such American staples as beef and coffee bought at the market. Learning how to cook some basic Japanese dishes using tofu, fish, rice, and fresh vegetables will keep your budget down and keep you healthy and satisfied. "The stories about $125 melons are true," says Victoria. "But nobody in Japan would buy them to eat for themselves. Businessmen buy them as gifts for their guests."

Hard work definitely pays off in Japan. And it is still possible to amass a modest fortune through teaching, although not if you limit yourself to the private language schools. "If you work at a school, you might get a flat rate of 3,000 yen an hour," says Victoria. "But if you are creative, you can find better situations. I was able to negotiate some great jobs. I saved $1,000 a month, and I didn't have a grueling schedule." Victoria saved more than $10,000 in nine months. But veteran teachers stress that it takes time to develop the personal network and savvy leading to the better jobs. "When I first got to Japan, I wanted to make as much money as I could," says Chris. "I worked all the time. I accepted any job offer, no matter how far I had to travel for it. I did earn money, but I felt that I should be earning more. I eventually started to hear about better jobs, and I realized that while I was teaching for $10 an hour, I should have been trying to line up more profitable jobs for myself."

No matter how hard you're working, veteran teachers emphasize the importance of looking beyond your job and your American friends and becoming involved with aspects of Japanese culture. It's quite easy to get lost in the quest for profit and to spend your limited spare time with other foreigners. But people who follow this course tend to burn out quickly. "You start to feel that you are part of the stereotype," says Andrew, who worked in Japan before starting graduate school. "You feel like a cog in a wheel."

Even if you are working full force, find the time to learn something about the country. Sign up for some Japanese lessons or classes in one of the classic Japanese art forms, such as flower arranging or martial arts. Though traveling can be expensive, it's quite easy and extremely rewarding.

Be especially sure to escape to the countryside—to Northern Honshu, Mount Fuji, the fertile rice fields of Noto-
Hanto—to experience what's left of undeveloped Japan.
The Japanese Tourist Bureau is exceedingly helpful and
efficient, and their elaborate brochures and booklets make
it simple to plan trips around the country. You should also
take advantage of their home stay program, which allows
you to spend time, from a few hours to a few weeks, with a
Japanese family at their home.

GETTING A WORK VISA

Japan's policy on granting work visas is time consuming
and inconvenient. But it's not as bad as the policy followed
by the United States, and since there is no way to get
around it, try to make the best of it. You should travel to
Japan on a tourist visa, which is valid for 90 days. This will
give you more than enough time to find a job. In order to
qualify for a work visa, you must find an employer willing
to sponsor you. As long as you have committed to teach for
at least 12 hours each week, your school should be happy to
sponsor you.

Sponsorship in hand, you must leave Japan to apply for
your work visa. Most people go to Korea (it's closest), Hong
Kong, or Taiwan. Once you apply for your visa, it takes a
couple of months for your request to be processed. So you
will reenter Japan on your still-valid tourist visa and begin
your life as a teacher. While it is illegal to work on a tourist
visa, most English teachers do it while they are waiting for
their work visa to come through, and few people have problems. Because the Japanese government is fully supportive
of the national campaign to learn English, they generally
don't crack down on English teachers.

When your visa is ready, you must return to the country
from which you applied for it to claim it in person.

LOW-COST ACCOMMODATIONS

Following is a list of hotels, pensions, ryokans, and dormitories that are popular among foreigners. They all have English—speaking staffs, and in addition to providing safe, clean, and inexpensive lodging during your first few weeks in Japan, they will put you in contact with the foreign community. Since all of these places are extremely popular, I have included phone numbers so you can make reservations before you leave the States. (It isn't terribly expensive if you call late at night.)

TOKYO
(To call direct to Tokyo, dial 011813 plus the seven-digit phone number.)

- **Kimi Ryokan:** 971-3766
  Rooms start at 3,500 yen per night.

- **Mickey House:** 936-8889 or 371-2252
  Rooms start at 1,300 yen per night.

- **Asia Center:** 402-6111
  Rooms start at 4,950 yen per night.

- **Green Peace:** 915-2572
  Rooms available on a monthly basis, starting at 38,000 yen for a dormitory room and 52,000 yen for a single.

- **Yoshida House:** 926-4563
  Rooms start at 1,500 yen per night.

KYOTO

(To call direct to Kyoto, dial 0118175 plus the seven-digit number.)

- **Tani House:** 661-2391
  Rooms start at 1,400 for a dormitory-style room, 3,000 yen for a single per night.

- **Kyoto Travelers Inn:** 771-0226
  Single rooms start at 5,000 yen per night.

- **Pension Utano:** 463-1118
  Rooms start at 3,800 yen per night.

- **Yuhara Ryokan:** 371-9583
  Rooms start at 3,000 yen per night.

- **Ichiume Ryokan:** 351-9385
  Rooms start at 2,000 yen per night.

For more information, contact the Japanese National Tourist Organization (JNTO), 630 Fifth Avenue, New York, New York 10111 (212) 757-5640.

RECOMMENDED READING

Japan: A Travel Survival Kit, by Ian McQueen. This travel guide will help get you over to Japan and keep you on the right track during your travels. ($12.95, Lonely Planet

Publications, 112 Linden Street, Oakland, California 94607 (415) 893-8555).

Japan Handbook, By J. D. Bisignani. A snappy guide to budget travel with specific emphasis on out-of-the-way places. ($12.95, published by Moon Publications, available by mail from Bookpeople, 2929 5th Street, Berkeley, California 94710 (800) 624-4466).

Jobs in Japan, by John Wharton, This friendly, lively book provides a great range of advice and hard information about finding jobs in Japan (especially teaching jobs) and adjusting to Japanese life. Its appendix includes names of more than two hundred language schools in Japan, plus cheap accommodations and recommended resources. ($12.95, The Global Press, 1510 York Street, Suite 204, Denver, Colorado, 80206) (303) 355-1311.

With Respect to the Japanese; A Guide for Americans, by John Condon. Written by a ten-year veteran of teaching in Japan, this book discusses Japanese society in terms of behavior and values. ($10, Intercultural Press, P.O. Box 768, Yarmouth, Maine 04096 (207) 846-5168.)

SUMMARY

Opportunities for Recent Graduates: There is a surplus of English teaching positions in Japan—with schools, corporations, businesses, individuals, and families. You can either head over their independently and easily land a job in Tokyo or Kyoto, or sign on with the Japanese Exchange and Teaching Program (JET), administered through the Japanese embassy in Washington, which recruits assistant English teachers to work in Japanese high schools.

Requirements: You do not need any previous teaching experience, but you must be a college graduate. Bring copies of your diploma or transcript, plus letters of recommendation from professors or previous employers.

Visa Information: You can fly to Japan under a tourist visa (do not mention that you intend to look for a job). Once you secure a job, you must leave Japan to apply for a work visa. Most people fly to Korea, Taiwan, or Hong Kong. It will take several months for your work permit to be approved, but you can begin working in Japan while you are waiting. Once your visa has been approved, you must return to the country in which you applied for it to pick it up.

Financial Arrangement: You must arrive in Japan with no less than $2,500 to cover your expenses while you are looking for a job and waiting for your first pay check to be processed (this can take up to one month). Teaching jobs in the private language schools pay an average of just over 3,000 yen ($24) per hour. Private and corporate jobs pay two or three times that amount but are harder to come by. Rents range from 40,000 to 100,000 yen ($300 to $750) and the cost of living is slightly higher than in New York City. You will have no trouble supporting yourself as a full-time teacher, and many people amass hefty savings. The JET program pays 3,200,000 yen a year ($27,000).

Time Frame: It takes several months to get settled as an independent teacher, and most people stay at least one year (many stay much longer). The JET program lasts for just under one year—from August to July.

How to Apply: Most people do not start looking for teaching jobs until they arrive in Japan. Jobs are advertised in English language newspapers (the Japan *Times,* Tokyo *Journal,* the Mainichi *Daily News,* and the Kansai *Time Out*), on bulletin boards at hotels, restaurants, and clubs frequented by foreigners, and by word of mouth within the foreign community. The JET program is administered by the Japanese embassy in Washington (2520 Massachusetts Avenue, N.W., Washington, D.C. 20008 (202) 939-6700).

Pros:

- Bountiful job opportunities.

- High salaries.

- Tight-knit community of foreigners.

Cons:

- Becoming isolated from Japanese culture.

- A high cost of living.

KENYA

WorldTeach
Phillips Brooks House
Harvard University
Cambridge, Massachusetts 02138
(617) 495-5527

Sixty percent of Kenya's young people seek their high school education at harambee ("self-help") secondary schools—small, locally run high schools that squeak by, in most cases, without any financial support from the government. The education available at a harambee school is deficient, while teachers are always overworked and often underqualified. Textbooks are scarce and school supplies are in such short supply that students often turn in homework assignments on scraps of newspaper and cardboard.

But for harambee students, most of whom are from poor farming families, it's harambee or nothing. Unable to afford tuition at the superior government secondary schools (or sometimes simply unqualified), these students know the harambee education as their one shot at a college education and a better life. Sadly, success is rare. Just two out of every one thousand harambee students find places in Kenyan universities. A few more make it to a teacher training college. But despite the odds, the atmosphere in the harambee classroom is serious and hopeful. Students, whose parents scrounged for their tuition, are diligent, and teachers are dedicated.

This is the climate of the WorldTeach experience. As a WorldTeach volunteer, you will spend one year teaching English, math, or science in a harambee school in western Kenya. And while you can't expect to forge lasting changes in the harambee system, your daily efforts, according to former WorldTeach volunteers, will be deeply appreciated by your students and fellow teachers, and also prove quite rewarding for you.

WorldTeach is a program sponsored by Harvard University's social service organization, Phillips Brooks House. You don't need any teaching experience to qualify, although the program is intended for people who have a serious interest in teaching. "I didn't have any previous experience, so much of it was learning on the job," says Joseph, a Notre Dame graduate who served in WorldTeach before entering medical school. "In retrospect, I do wish I had had some training. The students work so hard that you feel bad about shortchanging them. This is a real job, and people shouldn't come here to play around. That attitude shows a very serious disrespect for the students, who work extremely hard, and their parents, who make big sacrifices to pay for their children's education."

Kenya is not a wealthy country. But it has been spared from the poverty that afflicts Uganda, Tanzania, Sudan, and other African countries. It has a fertile farm belt, some pockets of industry, and a healthy tourist trade. It also happens to be a beautiful place—with white-sand Indian Ocean beaches to the east; sweeping deserts to the north; rugged mountains which include Africa's second highest peak, Mount Kenya; a lively capital city, Nairobi; and spectacular game reserves.

WorldTeach volunteers are concentrated in farming villages that dot the western region of the country. In a typical village, as Jena, a Harvard University graduate and former WorldTeach volunteer describes: "There are farms scattered all around, and there might be a center area with a school, a drug dispensary, a place to grind corn into flour, a small market area, and maybe a bar." You will probably live near your harambee, in a one- or two-room house made of mud or cement. Lamps and stoves are powered by kerosene, and toilets and showers are usually in the backyard. "A good thing about WorldTeach is that you're a foreigner but you are living under basically the same conditions as the people around you," says Jena. "I lived with another volunteer in a cement blockhouse with an iron sheeting roof, two rooms, a sitting area, a cooking area and a latrine and bathing area out back."

Days start early (this is rooster country), and after a breakfast of tea and mendazi, Kenya's version of the donut, you'll probably be at school by 7:30 or 8:00. A typical harambee consists of one or two cement block structures with dirt or cement floors and thatched roofs. ("Birds fly in all the time," says Jena.)

Since harambee education is geared toward preparing students for college entrance exams, classes tend to adhere to facts and figures that students can memorize. Your students, seated in rows on wooden stools behind long narrow tables, will listen intently as you deliver your lecture and copy the lengthy note you've written on the blackboard. Classes tend to be small, but since discipline problems are all but nonexistent in Kenyan schools, larger classes are manageable. "They used to stand up and say 'Good morning, Madame,' until I told them to stop," says Jena.

School lets out in the middle of the afternoon, and unless you stay later to supervise a study session or soccer game, you'll be free to head home. Most WorldTeach volunteers work hard on lesson plans and take pains to return corrected exams and papers on time. For the most part, village life is free of stress. "I really liked the whole feeling of simplicity of life in the village," says Jena. "I liked getting up in the morning and having tea, walking outside and picking corncobs, hearing news on BBC, saying hello to people."

The fact that you are both a foreigner (rare) and a teacher (honored) will make you a welcome presence among your colleagues at harambee and your neighbors. Many of your free evenings and weekends will be snapped up. "People were always inviting us over for dinner and weekend trips," says Jena. "If someone invited you over at 10:00 in the morning, you couldn't count on being back until the evening." WorldTeach volunteers agree that the hospitality of the Kenyans is even more disarming than the physical beauty of the country, and sometimes even overwhelming. Joseph, for instance, was invited to the home of a watchman who worked at his school, a man with eight children and a pregnant wife. "He probably earned about $50 a month," says Joseph. Because Joseph had to return home before dark, he couldn't stay for dinner. So his host insisted that Joseph accept one of his few hens. "I tried to refuse but he kept insisting," he says. "There's an attitude there that you can't visit someone's home without being given something." A few months later, Joseph heard that the man's three-year-old son had died of malaria in a hospital 25 kilometers from his house. "He didn't have the money to bring his son's body back by vehicle, so he carried it on his back for 25 kilometers. I couldn't believe that this man had given me a hen."

You will have one month off between school terms, time you can use to return to the United States or to see something of Kenya, which is the preferred choice for most volunteers. Travel in Kenya is safe ("I hitchhiked all over Kenya and I would never hitch anywhere in the United States," says Jena). Good roads and cheap transportation make it easy to get to the area's bountiful game reserves, like Masai Mara (which borders Tanzania's Serengeti); the beaches and beautiful lakes, like Victoria and Turkana; and spectacles like Mount Kilimanjaro over the Tanzanian border. The most popular mode of transportation is the matatu, a private minibus fashioned out of pickup trucks and a few wooden benches, that zip around Kenya at high speeds. Despite a bad accident record and crowded conditions, matutus remain the vehicle of choice among WorldTeach volunteers and other budget travelers. "I just closed my eyes and didn't think about it," says Jena.

Staying healthy is a challenge in any Third World country, and former volunteers stress the importance of following a vigilant health plan. "I went running in shorts at six every morning, which was something they told me I just couldn't do," says Gena. "But I felt I had to. At first I was running in a skirt, but shorts were more comfortable and there were very few people out at that time anyway." Fruits, vegetables, and grains are plentiful, and meat is cooked on special occasions. In addition to native fare like corn porridge, beans, and chipati (fried pita bread), most large markets carry Western staples like cereal (which you can eat with heat-treated milk, potable for several months), peanut butter, Sprite, and spaghetti. The most prevalent affliction among WorldTeach volunteers is digestive turmoil from contaminated food or water; but you can usually stave off this condition by boiling your water and swearing off unpeeled fruits and vegetables, as well as any remotely suspicious-looking cuisine. Malaria is another threat (Jena contracted it and recovered), but in this case, too, caution pays off. "I slept under a mosquito net and burned coils in my room every few days," says Joseph. AIDS is a serious problem in many African countries, where some researchers believe it is transmitted through heterosexual sex. So while hysteria isn't called for, extreme discretion is.

Your WorldTeach term will begin with a three-week orientation in Kenya. The three-pronged training program will cover basic Swahili, teaching techniques and cross-cultural training. This is also your chance to get to know your fellow WorldTeach volunteers (there are between thirty and forty in every group) some of whom will live within a short matutu ride of your village. "On the Fourth of July, we got together in my village and had hamburgers and beer," says Joseph. "It was wonderful because we hadn't had anything like that in eleven months. Even though the Kenyans are really friendly and I had Kenyan friends I could hang out and talk with, it was nice to be with some other Americans . . . to talk about the election and nothing in general."

You will hear many languages in Kenya. English is the official language and the language used in schools. Your neighbors will speak either Swahili (the national language) or one of about forty-eight tribal languages. English will serve you fine in most cases, and the basic Swahili you will learn during orientation will get you through the market.

WorldTeach differs from some other volunteer programs in that you are responsible for financing your experience. The cost—$3,450—is low, considering that it covers round-trip airfare, room, board, and health insurance. But it doubtlessly discourages some qualified applicants (as well as some unqualified thrillseekers).

WorldTeach sends volunteers to Kenya three times a year—in April, August, and December. Applications are accepted all through the year. WorldTeach now also sends teachers to Botswana and China.

SUMMARY

Who They Are: WorldTeach, a program sponsored by Harvard University's social service organization, Philips Brooks House, sends American college graduates to teach overseas.

Opportunities for Recent Graduates: Recent college graduates can spend a year in Kenya teaching English, math, or science in a local "harambee" high school.

Financial Arrangement: Volunteers must pay a fee of $3,450 before leaving the United States, which includes roundtrip airfare, housing, food, insurance, and other expenses. You should bring along an extra $1,000 for incidental travel.

Time Frame: WorldTeach volunteers must commit for a minimum of one year, and have the option of extending for a second year.

Number of Positions: WorldTeach places approximately 100 people a year.

How to Apply: WorldTeach accepts applications year-round for departures in April, August, and December. The program is not competitive, although standards are rising.

Pros:

- High value of education in Kenyan society.

- Motivated students.

- Warm, welcoming people.

- A beautiful country.

Cons:

- Lack of teacher training for inexperienced volunteers.

- Health risks.

- Isolation from other Americans.

> **Travel Opportunities:** Many volunteers travel throughout the region during the one-month break between school terms. Travel is cheap, easy, and safe. Particularly notable destinations include the game reserves at Masai Marva National Park (over the Tanzanian border), the Indian Ocean beaches, the capital city of Nairobi, Lake Turkana, and Mounts Kenya and Kilimanjaro, also in Tanzania.

MEXICO

Los Niños
1330 Continental Street
San Ysidro, California 92073
(619) 661-6912
Contact: Volunteer Coordinator

From their San Ysidro, California headquarters (within eyeshot of the Mexican border), Los Niños has been helping orphans and families living in Mexico's impoverished border communities since 1974. In addition to its staff of Mexicans and Americans, Los Niños has close to twenty volunteers working in and around Tijuana, Tecate, and Mexicali.

Los Niños is one of the few organizations that has volunteers working on the front lines of Mexican poverty. The countless religious organizations scattered throughout the

country are generally open only to Christians, and the
Peace Corps doesn't operate in Mexico. Most Los Niños volunteers live in group houses on the Mexican side of the
border. And whether they're working in orphanages or in
the colonias (slum communities) with women's groups or
families, they are closely involved with the communities in
which they live. The work, according to volunteers, is interesting and satisfying. But most agree that it's the cultural
contact that makes the experience so enriching. "Living in
another culture and seeing how other people live encourages lots of growth," says Fred, one Los Niños volunteer.

The focus of most of Los Niño's activities is seven different orphanages scattered throughout the border area. In
terms of food, clothing, and health, these orphanages provide better care than many families can. Indeed, many children living in the orphanages were placed there by their
own parents, who couldn't support them adequately (some
children go home on weekends). But while the orphans are
clean and healthy, they lack the kind of individual emotional support they'd get from their own family. This is one
of the areas to which Los Niños volunteers can contribute.
"The kids aren't deprived materially," says Fred. "What
they need is affection. They're deprived of human contact."

Volunteers who work in the orphanages help children
with their homework, coach sports, and teach classes designed to train the older children in some marketable skill,
such as typing or familiarity with computers. They also
help the orphanage staff with general maintenance and
construction.

Outside of the orphanages, Los Niños volunteers work
with mothers of young children and families on a variety of
different projects that foster self-reliance among those who
are being helped. Shauna, who is volunteering before heading to medical school, set up a nutrition program for mothers of young children living in Mexicali. She conducts a
seminar on the basics of nutrition—the four food groups—

and a practical workshop in which mothers work together to prepare balanced diets for the children.

Fred is one of the many volunteers involved in a gardening project which helps families develop self-sustaining vegetable gardens. These gardens of corn, squash, beans, and eggplant can flourish into prime food sources for these families. Los Niños provides seeds and planting materials, and volunteers share techniques that will allow the families to sustain the gardens on their own and at low cost. "I knew something about gardening from my childhood," says Fred, "and I've learned a lot while I've been here."

Other volunteers work with women's crafts cooperatives. Using materials provided by Los Niños, the women design and produce handicrafts that volunteers help them market in their own communities and potentially in the United States.

Los Niños welcomes volunteers from all backgrounds, and many are just out of college. "It's a great place to come and learn some concrete skills," says Fred. "But we're starting to change our policy. We used to accept volunteers first and then look for ways to fit their skills in with our needs, and now we're evaluating our own needs first." A requirement that is now more stringent is knowledge of Spanish. One volunteer recommends at least two years at the college level. "Knowing Spanish is really important," says Shauna. "I speak it, and every day I think about what an advantage it is."

SUMMARY

Who They Are: Los Niños offers relief and development assistance to orphans and families living in Mexican border communities.

Where: In and around Tijuana, Tecate, and Mexicali.

Opportunities for Recent Graduates: Volunteers work with children in orphanages, run nutrition courses for mothers with young children, form women's cooperatives, and help families plant self-sustaining vegetable gardens.

Financial Arrangement: Volunteers serving one year or longer receive room and board plus a stipend of $50 per month.

Time Frame: Three months to one year (although only long-term volunteers are entitled to financial benefits).

Number of Positions: Between 15–20.

How to Apply: There is no formal deadline or starting date. Contact the volunteer coordinator at the above address.

Pros

- Working with children.

- Developing close ties to native communities.

- Developing fluency in Spanish.

Cons:

- Working in impoverished conditions.

- Possibly having to commute between California and Mexico.

TAIWAN

TEACHING ENGLISH IN TAIWAN

Overseas Service Corps of the YMCA, Taiwan
International Division
101 North Wacker Drive
Chicago, Illinois 60606
(312) 977-0031 or (800) USA-YMCA

Over the last thirty years, the tiny Chinese island of Taiwan has transformed itself from a sleeping farming society to a manufacturing and trade giant. And like their industrialized Asian counterparts in Japan and South Korea, the Taiwanese have an appetite for English that has grown along with their country's role in world business. Foreign language schools have flourished across the island, especially in its capital, Taipei, creating a beckoning need for native English-speaking teachers. For at least the past decade, Americans, Britons, and Australians have been able to land in Taipei, step off the street into one of many well-paying teaching jobs, and earn enough to support a lavish life-style (by Taiwanese standards), complete with Mandarin lessons and frequent trips to Taiwan's numerous natural and historic wonders. "I had a blast," says Andrew, who spent more than a year in Taiwan after graduating from college. "I had plenty of money in my pocket, I ate out every night, really good meals. I tasted about every dish available in restaurants in Taipei. I taught for three hours each night and had the whole day free. And I did a lot of traveling."

With the increasing number of teachers flocking to Taiwan in the last several years, competition for the plum English-teaching jobs has gotten stiffer, as is also true in Tokyo and Seoul. But if you are industrious, the independent teacher/traveler life-style is still viable, and for many, quite rewarding.

If, however, you are looking for a more in-depth cultural experience, you should forget about the independent teaching route and sign on with the Overseas Service Corps of the YMCA. As a Y volunteer, you will still be teaching English; but in addition, you will be a staff member of a close-knit Taiwanese YMCA and intensely involved with your host community. What's more, you have the opportunity to live with a Taiwanese family.

The YMCA's presence in Taiwan goes back to just after World War II. Today there are eight YMCAs scattered throughout the island—from Taipei to the historic Tainan to the boomtown Kaohsiung. And they all operate like those in the U.S.—as family-oriented establishments that offer a variety of learning programs to their members. For working parents, the YMCA offers quality day care. For teenagers, the Y offers leadership and sports programs. And for the growing number of Taiwanese who have discovered such luxury items as butter and ice cream, the Y offers fitness programs, which are quickly catching on.

But the most popular YMCA offering, by far, is English instruction. Although its classes are geared toward all levels of students, most are adults—business executives arming themselves with a tool for advancement, high school students hoping to apply to British and American colleges, and housewives continuing their educations. The Y prides itself on the high quality and low cost of its English classes, but it can't afford to pay teaching salaries that are compet-

itive with those offered by private language schools. So the
Y imports its own teachers from the United States, people
who are willing to accept less remuneration in exchange
for handsome cultural rewards. The pay, $425 per month,
is low compared to what you could make at the language
schools (although it's enough to support you). And the
hours are long—twenty hours of teaching each week plus
participation in other Y programs and social events. "Don't
be surprised if it's a Friday night and you are at work
hanging up decorations for the Halloween party," says Carolyn, a former Y volunteer. But given the welcome and
support you receive from fellow Y staffers, your Chinese
family, and Y students, most volunteers agree it's a worthwhile trade—off. "You instantly have a bond," says Carolyn.
"I was never without friends and something to do. The
Chinese open their hearts and homes to us, and you can
really become a part of their lives."

Your English classes, which will usually take place in
the evenings, emphasize conversation. "We touch on grammar points throughout the lessons, but we don't drill on
that," says Carolyn. "Most of your students have had that
their whole lives. You want to teach them to communicate,
to take risks, to open their mouths and start using the
language."

Any previous teaching experience will give you an edge
during the application process, which is somewhat competitive (forty out of two hundred were accepted in 1988). And
if you are hoping to be placed in Taipei, where the standards are more rigorous, you should definitely have some
classroom time under your belt. But for placements in other
areas, experience is not necessary. What's most important
is show of commitment. "It's not fair to have someone with
a lukewarm commitment," says Carolyn. "There is a high
regard for the teaching profession in Taiwan. The students
are very diligent. They prepare their homework. They
really want to learn. They'll be disapointed if a teacher

doesn't show up for class. They won't be satisfied to just take a walk or go home. They'll want to make it up."

For the initial three months of your year of service, you will live with a Chinese family, an arrangement that lets you adjust to Taiwanese life while you are learning about it. After those three months, you have the option of finding an apartment or room of your own or continuing living with the family. Most volunteers opt to stay with their family, and agree that the benefits overshadow the lack of privacy (you will have your own room, but accommodations tend to be crowded). Just how involved you are with your host family depends on what you are comfortable with. Many volunteers become entrenched in the household routine, returning home for dinner between evening classes and accompanying the family on outings and vacations. Other volunteers prefer a more independent arrangement.

Your teaching schedule and Y-related activities will fill up your week, but weekends and school vacations are open for travel around the island. Although many of Taiwan's cities bear the scars of rapid growth and industrialization, there are many remote areas—beaches, mountains, and forests—that are relatively untouched. Additionally, the tide of conservationism is gaining strength. There are some lovely beaches in the south near Kenting (covered with yellow coral sand) and some prime hiking spots in the northeast, especially in the mountains near Tokulo Gorge, which is itself one of Taiwan's biggest tourist attractions. You can enjoy the most striking scenery in Taiwan (some say in all of Asia) on the train ride from Chiayi to Alishan on the Alishan Forest Railway, which was built in the 1900s to serve upper mountain logging camps. The 44-mile ride will take you from sea level up to nearly 7,500 feet, from tropical forests to litchee orchards to the cypress forests of Taiwan's most famed resort, Alishan.

In addition to the lushness of its natural sites, Taiwan has a rich culture that reflects both its population of mainland Chinese, who came to Taiwan to escape Communism in 1949, and the native Taiwanese, who arrived from southern China about three hundred years ago. Buddhist and Confucian temples abound, and The National Palace Museum just outside Taipei contains the largest collection of Chinese art in the world, most of which was exported from the mainland when Communism took hold. For a dose of pure Taiwanese culture, take a walk down Taipei's Snake Alley any evening to see brothel-goers imbibing such aphrodisiacs as the blood of live snakes and turtles (the reptiles are slit open and drained while you wait).

While the Y program is not characterized by lavish perks, there are a few generous extras, like Y-subsidized Mandarin Chinese lessons and a free plane ticket back to the States if you successfully complete your term (95 percent of all participants do). At the six-month point, the Y will hand you a round-trip plane ticket to Hong Kong and a week's worth of spending money. Although the purpose of your trip is to renew your visa, it's also a paid vacation.

SUMMARY

Opportunities for Recent Graduates: The YMCA recruits Americans to join the staff of Taiwanese YMCAs. You will teach English and participate in YMCA fitness, social, and community activities. You will also live with a Taiwanese family (mandatory for the first three months, optional after that).

Financial Arrangement: The monthly salary is approximately $425 per month plus free housing. Volunteers must pay their airfare to Taiwan, but those who successfully complete the program receive a free ticket back to the United States. After six months of service, the YMCA provides volunteers with a free round trip ticket to Hong Kong and one week's worth of spending money. In addition, the YMCA will subsidize Mandarin Chinese lessons.

Time Frame: Volunteers serve for one year, beginning in either July or October. A second year is negotiable.

How to Apply: Applications are accepted year-round. Contact the YMCA office in Chicago for information.

Pros:

- Support and friendship from native Y staffers, community members, and a Taiwanese host family.

- Varied work responsibilities.

- A scenically beautiful country with a rich culture.

Cons:

- Relatively low salary.

- Long working hours.

Travel Opportunities: In addition to the one-week vacation in Hong Kong halfway through your term, you will have many opportunities to travel in Taiwan on weekends and vacations. Taiwan offers a fascinating culture that reflects both its native Taiwanese and mainland Chinese populations, plus many areas of scenic beauty.

MULTINATIONAL PROGRAMS

CAMPHILL CENTERS ABROAD

Below is a partial list of the Camphill villages and schools around the world. (See page 119 for a full description of the Camphill movement.) With seventy centers in sixteen countries worldwide, I couldn't include the complete list, but you can obtain one by writing or calling any of the centers. The following are those schools and villages most often recommended by Camphill residents.

Each center has its own admission policies. But in general, you shouldn't be daunted by the language barrier. As Maggie, a staff member at Scotland's Newton Dee Village said, "I can't tell you how many of the volunteers passing through here don't speak a word of English."

In addition to addresses, I've included phone numbers, including country code. In most cases you can dial direct, but it's helpful to call the operator for specific dialing instructions.

- **AUSTRIA**
  Camphill Liebenfels
  Sozialtherapeutische Werk and Wohnstatten
  A 9556 Liebenfels-Karnten Austria
  Phone Number: (Country code 43) 4215 48175

- **BRAZIL**
  Angaia Camphill do Brasil
  Rua Marechal Deodoro, 1155/104

C.P 1122, 36100-Juiz de Fora-MG Brazil
Phone Number: (Country code 55) 32 211 7507

● CANADA
Camphill Village Ontario
RR #1
Angus, Ontario OLM 1 BO
Phone Number: (705) 424-1162

● ENGLAND
Adult Community
Botton Village
Danby, Whitby
North Yorkshire Y021 2NJ, England
Phone Number: (Country code 44) 287 60871

Children's School
Sheiling Community
Ringwood
Horton Road, Ashley
Ringwood, Hants. BH24 2EB, England
Phone Number: (Country Code 44) 425 477488

● FINLAND
Sylvia-Koti
SF 16999 Lahtim, Finland
Phone Number: (Country Code 358) 18 878332

● FRANCE
Foyer de Vie
Le Beal

F 26770
Toulignan, France
Phone Number: (Country Code 33) 75535533

● GERMANY
Children's School
Heimsolderschule Brachenreuthe
D 7770 Uberlinger, Germany
Phone Number: (Country Code 49) 7551 8007

Adult Village
Camphill Dorfgemeinschaft
EV Lehenhof
D7774 Deggenhausertal 2, Germany
Phone Number: (Country Code 49) 7555 8010

● IRISH REPUBLIC
Camphill Community
Ballytobin
Callan, Co. Kilkenny, Ireland
Phone Number: (Country Code 353) 56 25114
ext. 21

● NORTHERN IRELAND
Gleneraig Community
Craigavad, Holywood, Co.
Down TB18, ODB, Ireland
Phone Number: (Country Code 44) 2317 3396

● NETHERLANDS
Stichting Christoporus
Bosch en Duin

Huize Kaspar Duinweg 35, The Netherlands
3735 LC
Phone Number: (Country Code 31) 3404 31904

- NORWAY
  Hogganvik Landsby
  N 4210 Vikedal, Norway
  Phone Number: (Country Code 47) 4760111

- SCOTLAND
  Adult Community
  Newton Dee Community
  Newton Dee, Bieldside
  Aberdeen AB1 9DX, Scotland
  Phone Number: (Country Code 44) 224 868701

  Children's School
  Camphill Rudolf Steiner Schools
  Murtle, Bieldside,
  Aberdeen AB1 9EP, Scotland
  Phone Number: (Country Code 44) 224 867935

  School for Teens
  Templehill Community
  Gelnfarquhar Lodge
  Kincardineshire AB3 1UJ, Scotland
  Phone Number: (Country Code 44) 5612325

- SWEDEN
  Staffansgarden/Mickelsgarden
  Furugatan 1

S 82060 Delsbo, Sweden
Phone Number: (Country Code 46) 653 10807

● SWITZERLAND
Village Aigues-Vertes
CH 1233 Chevres-Bernex,
Geneve, Switzerland
Phone Number: (Country Code 41) 22571721

● WALES
Coleg Elidyr
Rhandirmwyn
Nr. Llandovery,
Dyfred SA 20 ONL, Wales
Phone Number: (Country Code 44) 5506 272

Council on International Educational Exchange
205 East 42nd Street
New York, New York 10017
(212) 661-1414

In most countries, the policy on granting work permits to Americans is governed by a simple Catch 22: you can't get a permit without first getting a job, and you can't get a job without first getting a permit.

Fortunately, there is a program sponsored by the Council on International Educational Exchange (CIEE) that eliminates this problem for students and recent graduates who want to work in Great Britain, Ireland, France, West Germany, New Zealand, and Costa Rica. CIEE has worked out an exchange arrangement between the United States and each of these countries which allows a certain number of Americans to work abroad and a certain number of foreign young people to work in the United States. Last year, more than five thousand Americans worked abroad through the CIEE program.

The program is extremely simple, You fill out a CIEE application, and usually within a month or so, you will receive your permit. Nearly everyone who applies is accepted, and while CIEE can't guarantee you a job once you arrive, your prospects are extremely good. Your program fee of $82 entitles you to full use of the employment resources of CIEE's cooperating agency in your host country, and according to CIEE records, the vast majority find jobs within three days of their arrival.

There are two limitations to this program. First, once you graduate from college, you have only one semester to use the permit. After that, you no longer qualify for the program, which is geared toward students. And second, the work permits are valid for only a limited amount of time:

Great Britain: Up to six months
Ireland: Up to four months
France: Up to three months
West Germany: June 1 to October 1
New Zealand: April 1 to October 31
Costa Rica: June 1 to October 1

The clock starts ticking the day you step foot in the host country.

Most CIEE participants go after clerical, restaurant, farm, hotel, and sales jobs—the kinds of jobs you might take in this country during the summer. Young Americans are secretaries in London, wind surfing instructors at the resorts of Dover, waitresses in Auckland, camp counselors in the Irish countryside, and sales people in the boutiques of France. "I worked for a large corporation as the secretary to the financial director," says Libby, who spent six months in London. "It was fun being a secretary because I knew that I wouldn't be one for the rest of my life."

Career-oriented jobs are also available, but obtaining one requires the same resourcefulness you would employ in searching for a job in this country. Writing to potential employers before you leave the United States is recommended. This approach landed one recent graduate a production assistant job with MTV Europe and helped a recent Harvard graduate arrange an internship with a prestigious London investment banking firm. CIEE's dossiers are filled with similar success stories. If you would rather not start looking until you arrive, bring along a professional resume and several letters of recommendation.

Whatever your job, you will be paid the same amount as your native colleagues, and on this salary most people have little trouble supporting their daily life and saving some money for modest traveling. At last count, secretaries were making $305 per week in London. ("It's considered highly skilled labor if you can type," says Libby.) Waiters were earning $155 per week in Paris, and farmhands were making $50 plus room and board in West Germany. You are responsible for paying your roundtrip plane fare (CIEE offers great deals on plane tickets), but many people manage to make that up in their jobs.

In addition to helping you find a job, CIEE's cooperating agencies will offer you leads on housing and advice on getting settled.

SUMMARY

Who They Are: CIEE is the world's largest organization dealing with international education and travel. In addition to organizing work, study, and travel programs for students, CIEE offers a wide range of travel services, including discount airline tickets, charter flights, student discount cards, and travel guides.

Where: CIEE offers programs around the world.

Opportunities for Recent Graduates: As a recent graduate, you are eligible for CIEE's work-abroad program, which provides you with a permit to work in Great Britain, Ireland, France, West Germany, New Zealand, or Costa Rica.

Financial Arrangement: The program fee is $82, which buys you a work permit and the employment resources of CIEE's cooperating agencies overseas. You should earn the same amount as your native co-workers, and you should have no problem covering both living and modest travel expenses. You are responsible for your roundtrip airfare.

Time Frame: You must use your work permit within one semester of graduation. Your work permit is valid for between three and six months, depending on the country:
  Great Britain: Any time of year up to six months.
  Ireland: Up to four months.
  France: Up to three months.
  West Germany: June 1 to October 1
  New Zealand: April 1 to October 31
  Costa Rica: June 1 to October 1.

Number of Positions: In 1988, more than five thousand American students worked abroad through CIEE's program.

How to Apply: Applications are available at CIEE.

Pros:

- Working legally in well-paying jobs.

- Simple application process.

- Varied job options.

Cons:

- Requirement of using permit within one semester after graduation.

- A time limit once you arrive in the country.

Peace Corps
806 Connecticut Avenue, N.W.
Washington, D.C. 20526
(800) 424-8580 extension 293
or (202)-254-6886

The Peace Corps is approaching its 30th birthday with renewed vitality. Recovered from the neglect it suffered in the more self-involved seventies and under the guidance of its current director, Loret Miller Ruppe, it is gaining new visibility, Congressional support, and vision. And although it may never recapture the Kennedy-inspired romance and idealism of its infancy, it will certainly continue to help people in developing nations and to offer excellent opportunities to serious-minded volunteers.

The Peace Corps is not for dabblers. It requires a 27-month commitment—three months of intensive language and cultural training followed by two years of service. This time frame allows for an experience of uncommon cultural depth. "You don't just learn about the country," says one volunteer. "You understand it." You will emerge stronger and probably somewhat wiser, because the Peace Corps, as any returned Peace Corps volunteer (PCV) will tell you, requires staying power.

There are currently 5,200 Peace Corps volunteers serving in 65 countries around the world. The volunteers are spread among three regions: Sub-Saharan Africa, Inter-America, which includes Central and South America and the Caribbean, and NANEAP, the acronym for North Africa, the Near East, Asia and the Pacific. The countries with the highest concentration of volunteers include Honduras (318), the Philippines (275), Guatemala (261), Costa Rica (221), Ecuador (218), Sierra Leone (190), Kenya (180), and Thailand (179). The smallest number are in the islands of the South Pacific, including Tuvalu, which has only one volunteer, and the Cook Islands, which has three.

Several factors influence the Peace Corps presence in a country. Most important, the Peace Corps does not go to work without an invitation from the host country. The host government also plays a significant role in shaping the size of the volunteer population and the types of projects the volunteers will carry out. The Peace Corps does not operate in countries at war or in major turmoil; it pulled out of Iran in 1976, Chad in 1977, and Nicaragua in 1979. It will, however, try to weather periods of unrest. Volunteers in the Philippines worked through Marcos' ouster and remain in Sri Lanka despite violent civil conflicts. The roster of Peace Corps countries is constantly growing and changing; recent additions include Pakistan and Cape Verde, and within the next year or so, the Peace Corps hopes to set up programs in China and Bangladesh.

Where (in the world) you end up serving in the Peace Corps depends mainly on which country happens to have an opening for someone with your skills and experience. Peace Corps funding and U.S. foreign policy put a firm ceiling on the number of volunteers in each country, so even after you are accepted as a volunteer, you might have to wait months for an appropriate placement to open up.

The range of Peace Corps projects is vast. And what you will be doing will depend on what you have to offer. There are Peace Corps engineers supervising bridge and road construction, Peace Corps doctors running health clinics, Peace Corps water specialists designing water treatment programs, and Peace Corps teachers restructuring school systems. But as a recent graduate, probably without much in the way of definable skills, you should expect to make more modest contributions—helping a group of families plant home gardens or build clay stoves, helping some teachers design an English course, helping a women's craft cooperative get off the ground, teaching a nutrition course for mothers of small children. Former PCVs stress the importance of realistic expectations. "If you are a nurse and are expecting to change nursing in Guatemala, you are going to be disappointed," says Dan, who served in Costa Rica.

The three months of Peace Corps training you receive at the start of your term is a crash course in living abroad. It takes place either in your host country or in a neighboring country, and you will be working alongside other beginning volunteers. During training, you will be primed in the culture of your assigned country. You will learn about gender roles and stereotypes, sensitive issues and political problems, proper manners and traditional customs. You will also take several hours of language classes a day (the Peace Corps teaches two hundred languages and dialects). Though Peace Corps training is highly praised by former volunteers, you should do some preparing on your own time, before you leave the United States. "Read anything you can about your country before you leave," says Kevin, who served in Costa Rica. "Find out about its history, its government, its customs, its currency, its food, anything you can. It will make you feel more in control when you get there."

Peace Corps representatives keep close tabs on you during the application process and training. But once you are in the field, you are basically on your own. It's up to you to find a place to live, meet your neighbors, figure out what you are supposed to eat ("I stuck to rice and beans for a long time until I learned how to cook some of the local vegetables," says Dana, who served in Tanzania), and perhaps most difficult, get going on your projects. This lack of structure, especially where work is concerned, surprises many PCVs. So you should plan on it. "Be prepared for ambiguity," says Kevin. "Don't assume that you are going into a situation where the people are waiting for you, eager for your help, looking forward to change and knowing all about what a Peace Corps volunteer does and doesn't do."

You will enter your site with a project agenda worked out by the Peace Corps representatives of your country. But in many cases, former PCVs agree, the projects you were sent in to work on are ill conceived, lacking in community support, or simply unfeasible. It then becomes your mission to find projects that are indeed workable, and to quickly reroute your energy. Dana, for instance, was sent into a small farming village in Tanzania to work on a grain storage study. She pursued the study for five months before she realized, quite by accident, that the local farmers were not interested in participating. "I was frustrated at first, but I rallied," she says. "I said to them, 'I have a lot of skills, just tell me what you need.' " She ended up putting more energy into other types of grain extension projects she had been working on and starting up a sewing course that became very popular.

If for some reason you are not able to identify another project in your site, the Peace Corps will often move you. "People always have the option to change sites," says Sandy, who served in the Philippines and is now working in the Peace Corps' Washington D.C. headquarters. "If a volunteer is physically unable to handle their site, if it's not working out, if they don't feel committed or weren't accepted, we can often arrange a transfer of sites." Adds Kevin, who changed sites midway through his term: "They want to put you in a position where you can be as effective as possible."

Having some fellow PCVs close by can make your initial adjustment easier and soften bouts of homesickness. The volunteers who arrived before you can be your teachers, and those whom you meet during training will be your companions as you go through the often tumultuous process of getting settled. These people will be your family, your support system, and your link to home over the next two years. "The other volunteers are the only people on earth who know what you are going through," says Kevin. "Being with them is your only method of reality checking, or making sure that what you are feeling and thinking is normal."

While spending time with other PCVs can be a great source of comfort, however, former volunteers suggest that too much contact with other volunteers (or *any* Americans) can hamper the assimilation process and ultimately dilute the Peace Corps experience. This is a particular problem for volunteers placed in high density areas, like many parts of Central America, where there might be a dozen volunteers in one town. "I thought I was going to be in the middle of nowhere," says Kevin. "I ended up in a town with ten

other volunteers. Two of them lived next door to me. And
the city turned out to be popular among North American
retirees."

Most important as you start to think about joining the
Peace Corps is realizing that there is no generic Peace
Corps experience. Each volunteer goes through something
different, a blend of the culture of the host country, the
leadership in the host community, specific work projects,
and perhaps most important, the volunteer's own person-
ality. And you might find that many of the stock images
associated with the Peace Corps—tiny, unspoiled villages
populated with colorfully clad natives, and huge civil projects orchestrated by a lone Peace Corps volunteer—bear
little resemblance to reality. Some volunteers do in fact
wind up in tiny villages; but others are placed in capital
cities or large towns where modern buses whisk them to
work, Big Macs and pizza are their nutritional mainstays,
and CNN is beamed onto their television by satellite. "A
lot of people think they're going to be wearing a loin cloth
in the mountains," says Sandy. "And they end up disappointed." Although former PCVs agree that any placement
is a potentially rewarding one, the gap between reality and
romantic preconceptions is a common source of disappoint-
ment within the ranks of the Peace Corps. For this reason,
among others, the importance of approaching the experience with an open mind cannot be overstated.

The Peace Corps salary hovers at around $300 per
month, which buys more in some areas of the world than
others (in some places it's actually a fortune). You
shouldn't have trouble covering housing, food, and incidentals on this budget. The Peace Corps pays for all medical
expenses (and if you sustain any sort of permanent injury
or illness, they'll pay for lifelong treatment), and provides
a generous vacation allowance.

In addition, you will go home with $175 for every month
you serve—roughly $4,725 for a 27-month term. In large

part, your lifestyle will be dictated by the standard of living and local customs in your site. If most of your neighbors live in mud huts or wash their clothes in a stream, so will you. "My village had one bad road leading to it, no doctor and no electricity," says Sandy. "Just getting to the market was a four-hour walk plus a three- to five-hour bus ride."

Though learning to live like your neighbors can be difficult, this parity is extremely important, both to your image ("They appreciate that you are trying to do without," says Sandy) and your ability to understand what the community needs. "I think that Peace Corps volunteers are perhaps the best informed about the world because they've lived there at a level most people live at, writes Peter, who served in St. Vincent, not at the high 'diplomatic level' of most Foreign Service personnel but at the level of the people. Where it really counts." And perhaps most significantly, your ability to adjust to life on a more simple, less material-oriented level can have long-lasting ramifications on your own values. "When I heard about the stock market crash, I was sitting on a bus traveling through Guatemala," says Dan. "At first, I started thinking about how many thousands of dollars I would lose if the whole economy crumbled. Then I suddenly thought to myself, 'So what? It won't ruin my life.' I was perfectly happy living in my little house, eating rice and beans every day. The Peace Corps gave me another set of priorities to look at, and even if you don't accept them all, you realize what is important to you and what isn't."

If you have a strong interest in a particular region of the world, let the Peace Corps know. They will be receptive if you should request Thailand because you can speak Thai, or Africa because you studied the cultures in school. They will also respect your desire to steer clear of certain places for political or social reasons. "I didn't want the Philippines because of Marcos," says Kevin, who applied in 1985. Countries that are rich in indigenous culture, like Thailand, Nepal, Guatemala, and Kenya, are especially popular among volunteers. But placements in these countries may be hard to come by. By the same token, other countries carry bad reputations for reasons ranging from inordinately high volunteer populations (Belize) to unappealing right-wing political leaders (Paraguay).

One of the more practical fringe benefits of the Peace Corps is travel, not merely through your host country, but through a surrounding region. Many Peace Corps projects include visits to other sites and workshops around the country. And though the Peace Corps doesn't encourage frequent junkets, you can certainly steal away a few weekends now and then. Volunteers in Thailand can travel to the breathtaking beaches, volunteers in Nepal can participate in a few Himalayan treks, and volunteers in Tanzania and Kenya can visit the game reserves.

Your best chance to travel, though, comes at the end of the term, when Peace Corps will pay you a third of your readjustment allowance and the cash equivalent of a plane ticket back home. For most volunteers, the trip home turns into a full-scale odyssey. Sandy, for instance, stopped off in Thailand, China, and Japan after leaving his site in the Philippines. And Kevin stretched his trip from Costa Rica to the United States over two and a half months, visiting Guatemala, Nicaragua, and Panama before boarding a U.S.-bound bus through Mexico. "Traveling home by land instead of just flying gave me time to think about my experience in the Peace Corps and to prepare myself for picking up my life in the United States," Kevin says.

As the Peace Corps has changed over the years, so has the profile of the average Peace Corps volunteer. Today's Peace Corps volunteers are somewhat older (the average age is 30), more skilled, and more experienced. But there is still a place for the recent graduate. The protracted application process that includes eight letters of recommendation, an essay, and usually a personal interview, will give you a chance to present a multifaceted image of yourself and what you might be able to contribute. "We look at your past commitments, like sticking out a job that maybe you didn't like and going to school at the same time," says Cecilia, a Peace Corps recruiter in Washington D.C. "We look for involvement in community service or a volunteer job that maybe wasn't that much fun, but one that you were committed to. We also look for social sensitivity, or how well you seem to understand the needs and desires of others."

Any type of personal volunteer experience shines through on a Peace Corps application. "That's really important because it shows that you go out and do things on your own," says Cecilia. If your recruiter doesn't think your application is strong enough, you might be sent out to do some volunteering before your application is formally reviewed. "Three to six months of experience will make you more competitive," says Cecilia.

Once you are accepted to the Peace Corps, it often takes months for a spot in your program area to open up. And former volunteers advise against making any major life changes before you get a firm destination and date from the Peace Corps. "For me it worked out perfectly," says Kevin. "I graduated from college and three weeks later I was in Costa Rica. But that's not typical. You might find yourself with a huge block of time on your hands. So don't quit your job or sell your car until you know exactly where you are going and when you're leaving."

In discussing their personal growth experienced in the Peace Corps, volunteers incline toward terms normally associated with Olympic athletes, Arctic explorers, and others whose rewards are inextricably linked to challenge and sacrifice. The Peace Corps will certainly challenge you. Twenty percent of those who enter leave before their term ends. But few volunteers emerge from the experience unchanged. And according to a Peace Corps poll, 98 percent would do it again. "Being a Peace Corps volunteer has changed my life," writes Charles, who served in Jamaica. "I can say that without being able to articulate how or why. I just know it has . . . and I'm happy with that change. Perhaps I can say it in this way: my sense of self-worth is much greater, my vision and perspectives are sharper, my spiritual growth is unquestioned. What has being a Peace Corps volunteer meant to me? Probably everything."

SUMMARY

Who They Are: The Peace Corps is a United States government agency that sends American volunteers to work in developing countries.

Where: In 1988, the Peace Corps sent volunteers to 65 countries in Central and South America, the Pacific, Asia, Africa, the Caribbean, and the Near East.

Opportunities for Recent Graduates: Although the Peace Corps is trying to recruit people with skills and job experience, there are many recent graduates in the ranks. Volunteers work on projects relating to small enterprise development, forestry and natural resources, health and nutrition, fisheries, agriculture, energy and appropriate technology, housing and construction, water and sanitation, and education. The projects you work on relate to your skills and experience.

Financial Arrangement: The Peace Corps covers all major expenses relating to your service, including airfare to and from your host country, approximately $300 per month to cover living expenses, plus all of your health care. You also receive a readjustment allowance at the end of your term—$175 for every month served, or roughly $4,725.

Time Frame: You must commit for 27 months—three months of initial training plus two years of service. Extensions are granted if related to your project.

Number of Volunteers: There are currently about 5,200 volunteers in the field, but the agency plans to increase that number to 10,000 by 1992.

How to Apply: The Washington headquarters will refer you to the recruiter nearest to you. The application process is long, involving eight letters of recommendation, a personal essay, and often a personal interview.

Pros:

- Great opportunities for personal growth.

- Intense cultural experience.

- Language fluency.

Cons:

- 27 month commitment.

- Lack of structure in your site.

- Working within a bureaucracy.

Travel Opportunities: Peace Corps volunteers can take weekend trips around their country and region and are offered approximately ten vacation days per year (this varies from country to country), which volunteers can use to travel home to the United States or through their country or region. But the best opportunity for travel comes at the end of your term, when the Peace Corps will pay you one-third of your readjustment allowance (approximately $1,500) and the cash equivalent of plane fare home. Many volunteers use this benefit for taking extensive journeys around the region.

WORK CAMPS

A work camp is a small, temporary community of volunteers from all over the world who work together to help a local community or organization. Over the past year, work camp groups have helped renovate a youth center on a Navajo reservation, turned a defunct reindeer farm into a community center in Finland, rejuvenated the James Joyce house in Dublin, and produced a video on tourism in the small Danish town of Vejle.

There are hundreds of work camps in operation each year, mainly during the summer months. Most last for several weeks and accommodate between 10 and 20 volunteers. Though Europe continues to host the vast majority of work camps, the idea is beginning to catch on in the United States, and there are a few scattered across Asia and Africa.

As a work camp volunteer, you exchange your full-time efforts for room and board. Accommodations tend to be rustic but safe and comfortable. The only requirements are a willingness to work and a desire to contribute to the community spirit.

Most work camps involve some sort of physical labor—building a school, painting a town center, clearing a field—but many camps combine work with study and discussion. Last year, work camp volunteers spent several weeks at a camp for conscientious objectors in Switzerland. They spent part of each day chopping wood for fuel and helping maintain the facilities, and the rest of the time learning about pacifism. Other work camps spring up to further an ideological cause, like helping an environmental group organize a blitz-mailing about acid rain.

The best way to get involved with a work camp is to contact two American coordinating agencies—Service Civil International (SCI) and Volunteers for Peace (VFP). Both organizations publish extensive annual catalogs of work camp offerings around the world and will help you register for the work camp of your choice. It's a good idea to read through the catalogs of both organizations before making your selections, although there is a great deal of overlap. Placements are made on a first-come, first-served basis, so make your choices early.

Since most work camps last only a few weeks, many people sign up for several and spend a few months hopscotching from one to the other. Not only is this an extremely cheap way to travel, but it will put you into contact with people you would surely miss as a tourist.

SERVICE CIVIL INTERNATIONAL USA

Route 2
P.O. Box 506
Crozet, Virginia 22932

Fees: $25 for United States work camps; $50 for work camps abroad. $15 for each additional work camp. $10 is refunded if you fill out a work camp evaluation when you get home. Room and board is free once you arrive at the work camp.

VOLUNTEERS FOR PEACE (VFP)

43 Tiffany Road
Belmont, Vermont 05730
(802) 259-2759

Fees: $10 annual membership fee to receive the catalog; $75 per work camp in Western Europe; $90 per work camp in Eastern Europe. You can deduct your annual membership fee from your registration fee. $10 is refunded if you submit a work camp evaluation when you get home. Room and board is free once you arrive at the work camp.

CHAPTER TWO

VOLUNTEER OPPORTUNITIES

Our generation is entering a world that is deeply troubled, a world whose problems—poverty, resource depletion, crime, drug abuse, racism—are overwhelming. We learn about some of these problems in college, we read about them every day in the newspapers, and we talk about them with our friends. But for most of us, the idea of trying to do something about them is too daunting. Some people label it apathy. I think, instead, that it's helplessness; we believe that there is nothing we can do to make a difference.

The fact is, of course, that we are not helpless and that these problems are not lost causes. And this is what working for any one of the organizations in this chapter will help you understand. These organizations are filled with people who are addressing problems and coming up with workable solutions. The Meadowcreek Project in Arkansas is exploring practical and academic answers to our environmental crisis. Camphill Villages throughout the world have designed a system of community that allows the mentally retarded to live up to their full potential. Jubilee Partners gets around America's strict policy on political asylum by helping Central American political refugees get into Canada.

These and countless other organizations around the world offer wonderful full-time volunteer and internship opportunities for recent graduates. Most of them will offer you room, board, and a small stipend in exchange for your fulltime efforts. You will work hard and live "simply," as program directors like to put it. But in return, you will be given a chance to learn and contribute in an environment that is vibrant and supportive.

The following opportunities are available in the United States. Chapter 1, Opportunities Abroad, includes volunteer programs in several foreign countries.

DEFERRING YOUR STUDENT LOANS

As a full-time volunteer, you are entitled to defer most student loans for up to three years. This privilege, which came about in 1973 as part of the Domestic Volunteer Services Act, is fairly far-reaching. There are a few hitches, however. First of all, you must be working for an organization that is tax-exempt under section 501-C3 of the IRS code. And you must be committed to that organization for at least one year. Most government loans apply, but the law gets fuzzy when it comes to private loans. Your best bet is to phone the Department of Education's student loan division: (202) 732-4242. They'll answer your questions and tell you how to proceed with your bank or student loan office.

LIVING AND WORKING WITH THE HANDICAPPED

Camphill Village Kimberton Hills
P.O. Box 115
Kimberton, Pennsylvania 19442
(215) 935-0300

Camphill Special Schools, Beaver Run
RD 1
Glenmoore, Pennsylvania 19343
(215) 469-9236

Camphill Village U.S.A.
Copake, New York 12516
(518) 329-7924

The Camphill Village at Kimberton Hills is a farm community set among fertile fields of rural southeastern Pennsylvania. The 130 people who live here are of all ages and backgrounds—families with small children and grandparents, executives and professionals on hiatus, recent graduates and European students on leave. Living and working together with remarkable openness, sharing, and mutual support, these people have created a vibrant community matched by few others in the country—even in the world. At the same time, they have fostered a productive, healing environment for the handicapped adults who live and work alongside them.

Camphill at Kimberton Hills is one of seventy Camphill villages, schools and centers around the world. At the most basic level, the Camphill movement means working with the handicapped in such a way that they reach their greatest potential. But just as important (or perhaps more important) is an unspoiled notion of community, the idea that all types of people can come together and through hard work and lots of understanding and support, forge a meaningful life-style that brings out the best of each individual, including those with mental and physical handicaps.

If you're cringing at the echoes of Utopia and the New Age, hold on a bit longer. Because while the philosophy that spawned the Camphill Movement can get quite rarefied, these communities actually work, not only for the handicapped, but for the thousands of other people, including scores of recent graduates from all over the world, who pass through each year. "The mentally retarded are the glue of these communities," says Helen, a long-time Camphill resident. "There are times we would have blown out of here if it weren't for the thought of who would cook breakfast for Willy and Peter."

The biggest problem you might encounter at Camphill, in fact, is getting yourself to leave after a year or two. "I came for a night 33 years ago," says Helen.

Each Camphill center has a slightly different orientation and focus of activity for its residents. Kimberton Hills, for instance, is a highly productive farm that practices Biodynamic agriculture, a method of organic farming that approaches each separate part of the farm—the soil, the plants, the animals—as part of one interdependent organism. Some centers are schools for children with autism, Down's Syndrome, childhood schizophrenia, and other mental handicaps. Other centers are artisan villages or practical training centers for adults.

But no matter which Camphill center you choose, whether it's in Ireland, Brazil, Finland, or New York, whether you stay for a few months or twenty years, you'll be actively participating in community living. And while the intricacies of life vary from place to place, there are some basic commonalities that can be drawn from the example of Kimberton Hills.

The centerpiece of Kimberton's 350-acre property is an imposing stone mansion fronted by white pillars which serves as the community office. It, like many Camphill facilities around the world, used to be the home of a wealthy estate farmer. ("We're good at taking over what rich people give us," says Helen.) The 130 residents, of whom roughly half are mentally handicapped, are scattered among thirteen houses spread erratically over a property of lush fields, flower gardens, and rolling hills. The houses, some new and some renovated, are all carefully designed to meet Camphill's architectural ideals: organic shapes, few angles, oceans of sunlight through huge windows and skylights. They are well furnished and filled with cozy touches, plenty of plants and artwork. Each person has a private room and everyone shares cooking meals and keeping the household clean and functional. Each household has a set of "houseparents"—usually long-term residents—who make sure standards of upkeep and decorum are met. The population of each house usually includes several mentally handicapped residents, a family, often with small children, and several single residents, short and long term, of varying ages. "Each house has a very different atmosphere," writes student Disa in a personal letter sent out to prospective Kimberton Hills joinees. "One's experience and perspective of Kimberton Hills is influenced to a large extent by where one lives, and each person's impact is felt very strongly in the common house."

At Kimberton Hills, running the extensive farm is a massive team effort with each person taking part according to their expertise and interests, but perhaps most important, the community's needs. In addition to the work around the farm—maintaining the fields, tending to the livestock or barns—there are jobs relating to the marketing of the farm products. The coffee shop, a sun-drenched room off the bakery, serves the public three days a week. The farm store sells beef from Kimberton cattle, fleeces from Kimberton sheep, baked goods, grains, and handicrafts produced within the farm community. "Some people come here with a specific desire to do social work; others come with the intent to learn about Bio-dynamic agriculture," writes Disa. "Whatever your motive may be, you will soon see that it is not possible to be exclusively involved in one aspect of the work. . . . A person may do anything from washing cow udders to organizing breakfast, welding a pig trough, harvesting beets, changing a baby's diapers, and listening to a lecture on Alexander the Great—and all of this in one day."

The official workday lasts until 5:00 P.M., and though household responsibilities might continue into the evening, you can always find time to enjoy the social and cultural side of life at Kimberton Hills, especially if you are among the dozen or so recent graduates and college students living here at any given time (usually hailing from four or five countries). There are singing groups, lectures, art shows and dances. And while you shouldn't expect to be hightailing it to Philadelphia every weekend, there are opportunities to venture out from time to time if you have a car or can borrow one.

At all of the Camphill centers, your room, board, and incidental expenses are taken care of for you. You're expected to arrive with a doctor's seal of approval, a solid set of teeth, and adequate clothing to withstand the extreme heat and cold of southeastern Pennsylvania. But if a medical problem comes up, you have to fly home suddenly, or your sneakers get eaten up in the garden, the community will take care of you. Even vacations, which are encouraged, are built into the community budget. Each center is financially independent and subsists through a combination of private donations and fees (usually paid by the families of the handicapped) and governmental support.

Another component of the Camphill experience is education. At nearly all of the centers, you can participate in a long-term training program in the applied teachings of Rudolf Steiner, the Austrian philospher upon whose concept of anthroposophy (the philosophy of man) Camphill is founded. Kimberton Hills, for one, offers a one-year apprenticeship in Bio-dynamic agriculture. Other Camphill centers offer rigorous three- and four-year programs dealing with working with the handicapped. These "training courses," or "seminars," as they're alternately called, concentrate on two slightly different Rudolf Steiner-based modes of working with the handicapped—Social Therapy and Curative Education. In both, you'll learn about the development of mental handicaps and a variety of innovative creative therapies, like art therapy, light therapy, and massage therapy. Even if you don't intend to stay the full three or four years (the degree, while not recognized in this country, is widely accepted abroad), the courses are worthwhile. "You can apply what you learn in the seminars to whatever you might do in your life," says Helen.

Of the ten Camphill centers in the United States, two others aside from Kimberton Hills are standouts for recent graduates. **Camphill Village, U.S.A,** in Copake, New York, is the largest center in this country, with two hundred people living on six hundred acres of wooded hills. This community revolves around handicrafts, although it also has extensive vegetable and fruit gardens. A bank of well-equipped workshops provide the residents (including the handicapped) with creative outlets and training in coppermaking, batiking, doll and toy making, woodworking and weaving, to name a few. And since some of the resi-

dents turn out some market-quality pieces, the crafts are
an additional source of financial support for the community. Copake also offers a topnotch training course in social
therapy.

Camphill Special Schools, or **Beaver Run,** in Glenmoore, Pennsylvania (eight miles from Kimberton Hills) is
a residential community and school for mentally handicapped children aged six to nineteen. For someone considering a career working with handicapped children, Beaver
Run is a chance to get a vivid preview. If you commit for a
year or more, you're given total responsibility for three or
four children. And as you may imagine, these children can
have tremendous needs, both physical and emotional.

During the school year, the children live at Camphill
(they return to their families over the summer). They live
among the staff members in ten bright and pleasant houses
on the property. Your assigned children will sleep in a dormitory adjoining your room, and you act as a parent, helping them get up, washed, and dressed in the morning,
making sure they eat their meals and get to classes and
therapy on time. You play with them in the evenings, take
them on outings, and stay up with them if they get sick.
"You don't have to know anything about handicapped children," says Tina, a houseparent here. "But you must be
interested in children, in the kind of liveliness and chaos
they bring to life."

At all Camphill communities, especially at those involving children, privacy is scarce. Although you have a private
room and time off throughout the week, there is rarely a
delineation between when you're working and when you're
not. A quiet afternoon of reading in your room may be sum-
marily interrupted by a crying baby or the watering needs
of a field of sunflowers. "I think most of us grow up where
we spend our day doing work that we don't like and then
we come home," says Tina. "But here, you might be working with the kids and having a great time. There's no sep-

aration. I really like that, but I know some people, especially college students, can feel overwhelmed."

The best way to begin getting involved with Camphill is to call one of the contacts listed above. Each community has its own admissions policy, but as Tina put it, "There's almost always room for one more." I found the staff members to be not only friendly and accessible, but also knowledgeable about the communities other than their own. So if you're not sure which one is right for you, they should be able to steer you in the right direction.

As for Camphill centers abroad, see page 95 for more information and a selective listing.

SUMMARY

Who They Are: The Camphill centers are residential communities where men and women of all ages and backgrounds live in a community with mentally handicapped adults and/or children.

Where They Are: There are seventy Camphill centers in sixteen countries around the world, with ten in the United States (see page 95 for Camphill Centers abroad).

Opportunities for Recent Graduates: Camphill is an intensely egalitarian organization, and recent graduates are welcome to join as short-term or long-term members of Camphill communities. As a resident or "co-worker," you participate in all facets of the community's social and working life.

Financial Arrangement: Room and board plus expenses are provided. You won't receive a monthly stipend, but all of your incidental expenses will be covered.

Time Frame: From several months to many years.

Number of Positions: Varies from place to place.

How to Apply: Applications are accepted at any time. Contact any of the above centers.

Pros:

- Vital, supportive community life.

- International volunteer population

- Unusual educational opportunities.

Cons:

- Lack of privacy.

- No clear delineation between work and leisure time.

Innisfree Village
Route 2
P.O. Box 506
Crozet, Virginia 22932
(804) 823-5400

Set at the base of the Blue Ridge Mountains, on four hundred acres of lush hills that burst into reds, yellows and blues in the spring, Innisfree Village is a thriving community. The 32 mentally retarded adults living here are valued, productive citizens who play a vital role in making this community run.

Like the Camphill communities after which Innisfree was modeled, Innisfree's volunteers and handicapped coworkers exist side by side. They live together, two volunteers for every six coworkers, in small houses. ("They're like the houses in suburban New Jersey," says one volunteer.) They work together in the village's weavery, bakery, woodshop, and garden. They prepare meals, take walks, watch television and take excursions to nearby Charlottesville. "These people are the most beautiful, happy people I've ever met," says Kate, a volunteer on leave from Brown University. "Our relationship with the coworkers is not professional; it's one of friends."

Working with the mentally handicapped can be rewarding in itself ("Even in the simplest tasks," says Kate). But what makes this place consistently rewarding for volunteers isn't just the work but also a community that is intensely egalitarian and cohesive. "Everyone has a say in what is going on, at every level," says Kate. "It was a real change from school, where you're only responsible for yourself, and not even that sometimes. Suddenly you're in the position where you are responsible for the next guy. It's scary to come into a group of 20 to 30 people and have to listen to everyone. But the returns are great because people are doing the same for you."

In general, coworkers are grouped in houses according to the kind of care they require. Volunteers living in houses with severely mentally retarded coworkers help with everything from bathing to dressing. In other houses, coworkers are totally self-sufficient. "Some have their own checkbooks," says Kate.

The days at Innisfree are full, but the pace is low-key. Most days begin at 7:00 A.M., with each household sharing breakfast. Work begins at 9:00 A.M., with coworkers, volunteers and staff taking turns manning the different workshops. The workday ends at 3:15 P.M. "There's a lot of flexibility outside the households and the work stations," says Kate. "In the afternoons, we have meetings, take walks, or go into town. In the evenings, we either spend time with the people in our households, or have a community activity, like a movie."

Volunteers don't need any previous experience working with the handicapped. ("I had never even shaken the hand of a mentally handicapped person," says Kate.) But for novices, adjustment can take time. "It can be a lot to handle at first," says Roger, another recent graduate. "There are a lot of basic things to learn, like who people are and what they're like under different circumstances." Adds Kate: "It took me a good six months to get the hang of it. But then all these returns started coming back. This is the most rewarding job I've ever had."

Innisfree offers its volunteers a generous benefit package —room and board, a $130 per month stipend, fifteen paid vacation days ($25 per day), and a readjustment allowance of $25 per month served. In addition, all volunteers get two days off a week. The minimum length of service is one year, but since staff turnover can be disruptive to the coworkers, Innisfree tries to recruit people who can make a long-term commitment. Volunteers currently working at Innisfree range in age from their twenties to their fifties.

SUMMARY

Who They Are: Innisfree Village is a residential village for mentally handicapped adults.

Where: Crozet, Virginia (twenty miles from Charlottesville).

Opportunities for Recent Graduates: Volunteers share fully in the lives of the mentally handicapped, including helping them with their daily routines, supervising them in daily work stations and accompanying them on outings.

Financial Arrangement: Volunteers receive room and board and a monthly stipend of $130, plus fifteen paid vacation days ($25 per day) and a readjustment allowance of $25 per month served.

Time Frame: Minimum of one year, no maximum.

Number of Positions: Approximately 25.

How to Apply: Applications are accepted year-round and can be obtained by contacting the current intern coordinator. Visits are strongly encouraged.

Pros

- Close-knit, egalitarian community life.

- Close friendships with the mentally handicapped.

- Beautiful rural setting.

- Generous financial arrangement.

Cons

- Total responsibility for caring for handicapped housemates.

- No clear delineation between work and recreation time.

SUPERVISING INNER-CITY KIDS

City Volunteer Corps
842 Broadway
New York, New York 10003
(212) 475-6444

The City Volunteer Corps is one of a growing number of state and local programs tapping into the energies of inner city kids to fuel community projects. The kids, most of whom are high school dropouts from poor backgrounds, earn a small salary and gain practical job experience and scholarship opportunities. At the same time, they reach out to hundreds of people and causes—the elderly, the physically and mentally handicapped, the young, and the city itself—that might otherwise be passed over by the city's overburdened staff and budget.

Working elbow-to-elbow with these kids are team leaders. People in this position (it pays $19,000 a year) are not volunteers, and they must have previous experience working with young people, such as being a Big Brother or Big Sister, a bike-trip leader or tutor. But being a team leader is extremely well suited for recent college graduates. Not only will you be taken on a whistle-stop tour of the range of community service work going on in New York City (as of 1988, the program had worked with 168 nonprofit and city agencies and served on 480 different projects), but you'll experience the challenges and rewards of working with young people from vastly different backgrounds. "In many cases, you're the first person outside of their neighborhood that has cared about them. And you can have a big influence in their lives," says Kenneth, former team leader and current staff member at the City Volunteer Corps. "You play a lot of roles in the kids' lives. You're a role model, a supervisor, a disciplinarian, and a counselor."

As a team leader, you will work with a group of up to thirty kids for one year (give or take a few dropouts and late arrivals), and accompany them to work assignments that last from one week to three months. You might spend two months tutoring elementary school kids in a low-income area of the Bronx and then two weeks helping plan a community garden in an abandoned lot in Manhattan's Lower East Side. "The assignments involving physical labor usually don't last long," says Francesca, a current team leader and recent Amherst College graduate. From there, the team might be called to deliver food to a group of homebound elderly people or to be counselors at a Brooklyn day camp.

Team leaders work the same forty hours a week as the young volunteers—usually nine to five. The intensity of the work varies from assignment to assignment. "We're

about to start at a daycamp in Brooklyn where most of the
kids are from a homeless shelter," says Francesca. "That's
going to be exhausting. But sometimes, the kids are assigned to different jobs and there's nothing left for the team
leader. And then the challenge is keeping busy." Rarely do
team leaders work overtime or have to bring work home
with them. "It's actually a good job to combine with graduate school," says Francesca, "not in the beginning, but once
you're comfortable."

CVC encourages each team leader to adopt a personal
leadership style. "Some get down and do the work right
alongside the volunteers, rebuilding playgrounds, parks
and housing for the homeless," says Kenneth. "Others prefer to just supervise, like foremen. They want to prepare
the kids for a real work situation. Either way, your number
one aim is to get these kids to perform quality community
service work, and it can be challenging to get kids just off
the boat from the Dominican Republic, black kids from The
Bronx, and white kids from Queens to work well together."

Methodology aside, the key to successful team management seems to be tempering the leadership role with
friendship and caring. And striking this balance can be
tricky, particularly for someone inexperienced in dealing
with young people. "The kids will test you in the beginning," says Francesca. "And you have to be tough. One of
the reasons I've been good at this job is that I can be firm,
but I'm friendly and I've established a lot of trust. The point
is to show them that no one can mess with you. Then you
can say, let's be friends."

Bonds between team leader and volunteers often take
time to germinate, and part of the job is accepting when the
chemistry just isn't there. "One of the hard things about
the jobs is when the kids don't respond," says Kenneth.
"You have to realize that you can't help everyone. I had
kids I just couldn't reach."

More often, though, team leaders and volunteers forge

close relationships. "When I first joined CVC, I had a young woman on my team who didn't want to go to school," says Francesca. "She and everyone else used to make fun of me because I was always saying 'You've gotta go to school, you've gotta go to school,' Well, I just found out that she got into college. I watch them grow up and I see that I've been an important relationship to them. That's been the best part of the job." Many of these relationships will continue outside the CVC. "I'm still in touch with kids from my team," says Kenneth. "You start relationships that last as long as you're a reasonable phone call away."

The team leader position is an obvious introduction for someone interested in pursuing community service or education. "You get a lot of insight of what is available," says Francesca. "Some of the things I see are depressing. But I work with a lot of people who care and that makes me optimistic about things." Team leaders agree that the personal and practical skills you develop on the job will serve you well on any career track. "I've become much more confident, as a leader, as a teacher," says Francesca. "I don't feel any barriers between myself and other people. I can talk to anybody now."

SUMMARY

Who They Are: The City Volunteer Corps places high school-aged volunteers in community service programs.

Where: All boroughs of New York City.

Opportunities for Recent Graduates: Team leaders supervise groups of young volunteers. They accompany them to each work site, monitor attendance and performance, and counsel them on personal, education, and employment issues.

Financial Arrangement: Team leaders receive a yearly salary of $19,000 for the first year, $20,000 for the second and $21,000 for the third year.

Time Frame: Minimum of one year.

Number of Positions: There are 38 team leaders.

How to Apply: Contact program director at above address or phone number.

Pros

- Chance to positively influence the lives of young people.

- Wide exposure to community service organizations.

- Varied work experience.

- Good salary.

Cons

- Gritty city environment.

- Need for extreme confidence and leadership.

- Daily reminders of seemingly intractable social problems.

LEARNING ABOUT PUBLIC POLICY

> **The Coro Fellows Program in Public Affairs**
> 95 Madison Avenue
> New York, New York 10016
> (212) 683-8841
>
> 1370 Mission Street
> San Francisco, California 94103
> (415) 863-4601
>
> 609 South Grand
> Suite 810
> Los Angeles, California 90017
> (213) 623-1234
>
> 4219 Laclede Avenue
> St. Louis, Missouri 63108
> (314) 531-1500

Over a recent nine-month period, Joe, a Boston College graduate, worked in the office of Manhattan Borough President David Dinkins, as well as for the Congressional campaign of Connecticut's Sam Gejdenson, the New York Foundation, WCBS-TV, and the New York State Public Employees Federation. It's not that Joe is fickle. On the contrary, his work experiences were carefully mapped out as part of the Coro Fellows Program in Public Affairs.

Founded in 1947, the Coro Fellows Program is designed to prepare promising people to cope with the complicated problems facing our public policy institutions—problems as diverse as housing shortages, AIDS education, foster care, and crime. As a Coro Fellow, you won't learn the answers to these problems. But you will come away with skills and experience that will allow you to more effectively confront problems in your own career, whether you go on to become the mayor of San Francisco (like Coro graduate Diane Feinstein), the treasurer of the United States (like Coro graduate Elizabeth Batov), or a movie critic (like Coro graduate Gene Siskel).

The program lasts for nine months, from September through June, and is offered in four cities—San Francisco (which has the oldest program), New York, Los Angeles, and St. Louis. Though you should submit your application to the center nearest your home, you may be placed in any of these cities.

For the twelve Fellows selected for each city, the Coro program is a vigorous blend of internships, seminars, retreats, group projects, and interviews. The foundation of the program is a series of full-time internships with five different organizations, each representing a different aspect of the public sector. You will intern with a government agency, a political campaign (timed to coincide with Election Day); a community agency; a corporation (so you'll see how the private sector is inextricably linked to the public); and finally, a labor organization.

Each internship within the program lasts approximately one month. Exactly what you do as an intern varies from organization to organization. Although many interns are greeted with meaty work assignments (for example, Dan, who is currently in the middle of his government internship, is writing the annual report for the San Francisco Municipal Transit Authority), your prime objective is to learn as much as you can about the organization—by observing, reading, and most important, talking to the staff members. "You get to talk to people who are interesting in and of themselves," says Joe. "It's very important to see that people working in city government have interesting, challenging jobs that they can make a good living at. Also, a lot of these people are risk-takers. And it's helpful to see that taking risks pays off. If gives you a sense of possibilities for yourself." In addition to the interviews during your internship, you will participate in group interviews with city officials, members of the media, and community and business leaders.

Twice a week, usually all day Friday and one weekday evening, your Coro group will get together for a seminar period led by a Coro trainer. "The seminars are very intense," says Dan, "and you are really expected to give a lot to the group." In informal discussions, role-playing, and structured exercises, you will drill on different aspects of gathering and assessing information, group communication, and creative problem-solving—all skills that you will refine during your internships. "When I go in to interview someone, I go in with two prongs of questioning," says Dan. "One set is geared toward getting the information I need for the project I'm working on. The second set is a Coro set of questions—about the organization, about where people fit in, how the organization is perceived. By the end of this program, I will have a lot of practice asking for information and judging whether it is relevant information. And I will be able to test information against the wide experience I have had."

The Coro Fellows Program costs $3,500. If you can't afford the payment up front, Coro will likely allow you to defer payment of at least part of it. Since you are not permitted to hold a job during the program, Coro also dispenses living stipends (which you do not have to pay back) of up to $10,000, according to need.

The program is open to college graduates of all ages and

attracts all types of people. A typical group will include at least a few recent graduates, but many Fellows are well into their 30s and 40s. With about four hundred people applying annually for 48 spots, the placements are quite competitive. If you make it through the first cut, you will be invited to participate in "selection day" in the city nearest to you. Most Coro graduates have vivid (though not always pleasant) memories of this full day of interviews and exercises. The general consensus is that the day is best approached with no expectations. "You can't cram for this," says Joe. "They're testing for real natural wits. It's not who has the best grades or who has done the most interesting things. It's who has natural smarts and can think on their feet," says Joe. "Just be yourself and have a good time."

SUMMARY

Who They Are: The Coro Fellows program prepares promising people for careers in public affairs.

Where: There are programs in San Francisco, New York, Los Angeles, and St. Louis.

Opportunities for Recent Graduates: As a Coro Fellow, you will participate in five successive full-time internships with organizations representing each component of the public sector—a government agency, a political campaign, a community agency, a corporation, and a labor organization. You will also participate in twice-weekly seminars, group interviews, projects, and retreats.

Financial Arrangement: The tuition is $3,500. If you can't afford to pay this up front, you can defer the payment until after you graduate. If you pay within one year of your graduation, you will not be charged interest. After that, you have four years to pay it back as an interest—bearing loan. You are not allowed to hold a job during the fellowship, but grants of up to $10,000 are dispensed according to need to cover living expenses.

Time Frame: The program lasts nine months, from September to June.

How To Apply: You should apply through the Coro center nearest you, although you may not be placed in that city. Placements are made with regard to the diversity of each group.

Pros:

- Exposure to many facets of public affairs.

- Meeting inspirational role models.

- Blending classroom learning with hands-on experience.

Cons:

- $3,500 tuition.

- Individual internships may lack structure.

HELPING THE HOMELESS

Community for Creative Non-Violence
425 Second Street, NW
Washington, D.C. 20001
(202) 393-4409

"I came here with a lot of misconceptions about homelessness," says Catherine, a recent graduate from England and
current volunteer with the Community for Creative Non-
Violence. "I saw them all as stereotypical down-and-outs. I
was shocked to find that homeless people don't fit into that
stereotype. A lot of the people at the shelter actually have
jobs, and are working hard, but they can't afford an apartment because there are no affordable apartments."

For a recent graduate who wants a crash course in the
complex problem of homelessness in this country, there is
no better training ground than the Community for Creative Non-Violence. This deeply committed advocacy group
has been addressing the problems of poverty and homelessness since 1970. They run one of the largest shelters in
America, the Federal City Shelter in Washington D.C.,
which provides food, shelter, clothing, medical care, and
counseling to over two thousand people a day. And they are
also extremely active on the political level. They lobby Congress on issues relating to housing and poverty, organize
national sit-ins and demonstrations, and generally draw
public attention to homelessness. "We don't think that just
offering someone a meal and a bed is enough," says John,

who left college in Virginia to volunteer. "We try to get to the cause."

Volunteers come here from all over the world. The current group of volunteers living on the shelter's third floor includes four Germans, two Danes, a Japanese, five Britons and a handful of Americans. The work here is hard, sometimes spanning seven days a week, well over eight hours a day. Often working side by side with shelter guests, volunteers are involved in all aspects of the shelter. They staff the medical and counseling clinic, supervise meal preparation, hunt down food, clothing, and furniture donations, and help their shelter guests get their government checks.

In addition to keeping the shelter running smoothly, volunteers can get involved in CCNV's political activities and community projects. Recently, for instance, volunteers befriended groups of children from a local welfare hotel. "The mothers are told by the hotel management that they'll lose their room if they don't watch the children themselves 24 hours a day while they're at the hotel," says Catherine. "So we'll take the kids on outings to give the mothers a break. We bring them to the beach, to Wildworld, and to the zoo."

CCNV policy gives volunteers free reign over their time. Ideally, this allows each person to devote themselves to the facet of the organization that most interests them, whether it's the political side, working closely with the guests or reaching out to the community. "Initiative," says John, "is the most important quality in a volunteer." This policy works well in most cases, but rookies should expect to confront a period of initial uncertainty. "It can be hard to know where you fit in at first," says Catherine. When I first spoke to Catherine, in her first month of service, she was at best tentative about the quality of her experience. "I really didn't know where I belonged," she says. But when I called six weeks later with some follow-up questions, she was deeply absorbed in a national protest CCNV was planning.

Her excitement was almost palpable. "This is an incredible place to be," she says now.

And despite some hard days, volunteers have time to enjoy themselves. "The evening meal is a time for us to be together," says Catherine. "And we go to clubs, or a Pink Floyd concert. A lot of us are on limited funds, so we go through the *City Paper* and find things to do that are free or really cheap."

Most volunteers live in private rooms ("Some are pretty big"), and meals are part of the package. But CCNV offers no expense for transportation money, so volunteers recommend arriving with at least a small amount of spending money to use on outings in Washington.

SUMMARY

Who They Are: The Community for Creative Non-Violence is an advocacy group that runs the Federal City Shelter, which offers a comprehensive range of services to the poor and homeless.

Where: Washington, D.C.

Opportunities for Recent Graduates: Volunteers are needed to work in all areas of the shelter—including the soup kitchens, office, medical facilities and social service center. Volunteers are also involved in CCNV's political activities and community outreach programs.

Financial Arrangement: Volunteers receive room and board, but are responsible for their own personal expenses.

Time Frame: Minimum of six months, no maximum.

Number of Positions: Ten to fifteen.

How to Apply: Volunteers are recruited year-round. Contact the current intern coordinator.

Pros:

- Addressing the homeless problem both practically and politically.

- The inspiration of working alongside CCNV founders and long-time members.

- International volunteer staff.

Cons:

- Living and working in the environment of a big-city shelter.

- No financial provisions beyond room and board.

- Minimal supervision.

BUILDING HOUSES FOR THE POOR

Habitat for Humanity
Habitat and Church Streets
Americus, Georgia 31709
(912) 924-6935

During the summer of 1987, three hundred men and women of all ages descended on Charlotte, North Carolina, stayed for five days, built fourteen houses for low-income members of the city, and then disappeared, returning to their lives all over the country. The organization responsible for this whirlwind of activity was Habitat for Humanity. The Habitat volunteer in charge was President Jimmy Carter. Not many of Habitat's projects around the country are led by former United States presidents (though President Carter has led several), and most are smaller in scope. But the Charlotte project was a dramatic example of what this Christian volunteer organization has been doing every day since 1976—building houses for people who need them.

Habitat for Humanity sponsors hundreds of building projects around the country and the world. All of them are staffed by volunteers. But the ripest opportunities for volunteers, particularly those just out of college, are in Americus, Georgia, the small town that's Habitat headquarters. There, amidst pecan groves and peach orchards (and a history as one of the centers of civil rights activism in the 1960s), is a year-round community of over one hundred volunteers and about twenty-five full-time staffers. Americus volunteers construct about twelve houses a year, and help administer Habitat's burgeoning activities worldwide.

Volunteers in Americus work a regular, forty-hour workweek. Only a small fraction of the jobs are construction related. The rest are administrative—from fund-raising to publicity to volunteer recruitment. Everyone lives, family style, in a neighborhood of houses near Habitat's office complex (which was constructed by volunteers). Housing is free and each volunteer receives $5 per week for food and $5 per month for expenses. "You can live off that if you're very, very careful," says one volunteer. Some long-term volunteers have part-time paying jobs in town.

But while the benefits are on the lean side, you'd be hard pressed to find a more vibrant community. Indeed, there are volunteers who have been in Americus for over ten years. And though this is a Christian-oriented organization, it attracts volunteers of all faiths. "People come to Americus for vastly different reasons," says Jack, who volunteered between college and medical school. "There are people who are just out of college, people who have just retired, people who are societal dropouts, and they're all sharing a life together."

SUMMARY

Who They Are: Habitat for Humanity builds inexpensive houses for low-income people in this country and abroad.

Where: Headquartered in Americus, Georgia (120 miles from Atlanta), Habitat has short-term and long-term projects throughout the country and the Third World.

Opportunities for Recent Graduates: Volunteers are needed at the Americus, Georgia headquarters in a wide range of jobs. Only about twenty of the positions are construction related. Other jobs include fund raising, public relations, project coordination, and general office work.

Financial Arrangement: Volunteers in Americus receive free room and $5 a week for food plus $5 a month for expenses. Financial arrangements vary in smaller locations. In some cases, volunteers must support themselves.

Time Frame: Anywhere from one weekend to life.

Number of Positions: Up to 140 in Americus, 100 abroad and thousands working in short-term and long-term projects around the country.

How to Apply: Positions are available year-round. Contact the current volunteer coordinator.

Pros:

- Large, varied, and vibrant community.

- Satisfaction of seeing construction projects through to completion.

- Low-pressure work environment.

Cons:

- Lack of privacy at home.

- $5 weekly food allowance.

HELPING POLITICAL REFUGEES

> **Jubilee Partners**
> P.O. Box 68
> Comer, Georgia 30629
> (404) 783-5131

The human rights records of Guatemala and El Salvador still rank with the worst in the world. But because their governments are considered democracies and share interests with the United States, political refugees—even those who have been tortured and threatened with death—have almost no hope of gaining political asylum in the United States.

So Jubilee Partners, a peace and advocacy group, helps these refugees get into Canada. Canada has a fairly generous policy concerning Central American refugees, particularly those with histories of oppression. And Jubilee Partners has helped scores of refugees start new lives there.

Refugees with strong cases for asylum are brought to Jubilee Partner's headquarters, a complex of modest buildings on 260 acres of lush countryside in Comer, Georgia. Refugees live on the property while Jubilee's staff presents their cases to the Canadian government. This usually takes two months.

Jubilee's property is, in itself, a lively, self-contained community. And it's here that the volunteers fit into the picture. The volunteers, an international group of about fifteen people of all ages, help keep Jubilee's community running smoothly. They staff the office, handle phone and mail queries, and maintain files. They work in the vast garden, planting and harvesting cabbage, carrots, beans, berries, broccoli, and other fruits and vegetables that are a main source of food for the staff and refugees during the summer months. They help promote Jubilee's other projects, which relate to such issues as banning the death penalty and aiding Central American amputees. And they chip away at the endless amount of carpentry, painting, and general maintenance going on around the property. "Our days are very diverse," says Lorraine. "Every morning, we meet in the dining hall, and whoever's doing work coordination says 'Here's what needs to be done.' And you choose what you feel like doing that day. Today I felt like working in the garden and I just got back from picking blueberries. Rarely do you get stuck with something you don't want to do."

The mood among volunteers tends to be social and supportive. They live together in a large, rambling house on one side of the property, where most rooms are doubles and meals and housekeeping details are shared. "I really enjoy it," says Bronwyn, a recent graduate of Colby College. "It's like a college dorm situation." And while the Jubilee community isn't exactly Disney World, seldom do volunteers seek amusement off the property. "You stay very busy here," says Lorraine. "You'd think that out there in the country everything would be very mellow. But there's always something to do. I wake up every morning happy and excited about being here."

The refugees have separate accommodations on the other side of the property. And while Jubilee's staff tries to offer them as much privacy and independence as they want, volunteers have many opportunities to spend time with them. There are frequent volleyball and softball games, and evening get-togethers like card games and dances. And many refugees opt to join the volunteers in the daily work assignments. "They have so many worries that some of them just want to keep busy," says Lorraine.

In order to spend more time among the refugees, many volunteers become English teachers. Spanish isn't necessary for teaching English, and Jubilee offers a crash English teaching course at the beginning of each volunteer session. "You get to know people really well through teaching," says Bronwyn. "And it's amazing how open and warm they are with us."

Jubilee is a Christian organization. Each day starts with devotions and there is a mass every Sunday. But they welcome non-Christian volunteers who are willing to "participate in the life of the community." And non-Christian volunteers say that they feel perfectly comfortable.

SUMMARY

Who They Are: Jubilee Partners is a peace and advocacy group that helps political refugees from Guatemala and El Salvador find political asylum in Canada.

Where: A 260-acre farm in Comer, Georgia (twenty miles from Athens).

Opportunities for Recent Graduates: Volunteers may teach English to refugees and participate in all aspects of running the community, including maintenance of buildings and property.

Financial Arrangement: Room and board plus $5 a week for expenses.

Time Frame: There are three volunteer sessions each year: January to May, June to August, and September to December. Volunteers may extend their stays, provided there is room.

Number of Positions: 15

How to Apply: Contact the current volunteer coordinator.

Pros:

- Sense of accomplishment when refugees are accepted into Canada.

- Close, democratic community.

- Low-pressure work environment.

- Peaceful, rural environment.

Cons:

- Small staff and volunteer population.

- Low-skill jobs.

LEARNING ABOUT ENVIRONMENTALISM

> **The Meadowcreek Project**
> Fox, Arkansas 72051
> (501) 363-4500

The Meadowcreek Project is a leading environmental think tank, research facility, and education center in rural Arkansas. Its small staff addresses the most troubling aspects of our deepening environmental crises—global warming, diminishing resources, soil erosion, and animal and plant extinction. But the main focus of its activities and programs is finding practical solutions. The project's guiding ideal is that of a "sustainable" society on earth—a society which recognizes that the earth's resources are precious and finite and respects the interdependence of all life forms. Project staffers pursue this goal with great creativity and hope.

Meadowcreek's approach combines academics with roll-up-your-sleeves practice. The staff sponsors annual conferences in which leading environmentalists, political scientists, theologians, and other scholars explore the academic and ethical underpinnings of our current environmental problems and consider possible solutions. The staff and guests live according to the basic tenets of conservationism: "Our day-to-day lives are very much oriented to being environmentally aware," says Allison, a former intern. "We turn off lights, use solar energy and composting toilets—

small things that would make a big impact if everyone was doing them." Meadowcreek's greenhouses, fields, and barns are proving grounds for environmentally sound farming methods. And the buildings on the 1,500-acre compound demonstrate the viability of renewable energy systems such as solar heating. "We really practice what we preach here," says David Orr, a former political science professor who founded the project with his brother Wilson.

The heart of Meadowcreek's activities is education. One of the brothers' prime concerns is that today's young people are ill-prepared to solve tomorrow's problems. Education, according to the Meadowcreek philosophy, must instill environmental values, and in order to do so it must cross the traditional lines between different academic disciplines. Every MBA candidate, for instance, should be required to take courses in ecology so that their future decisions—on where to open factories, how to dispose of their industrial wastes, where to build corporate headquarters—reflect an understanding and respect for environmental ramifications. And above all, education must instill students with a sense of caring about what they are learning. "Good education must help students go from 'I know' (cool professional competency) to 'I care' (competence plus commitment)," writes the Meadowcreek staff in a recent report. "This can be unnerving to many who equate the latter with a loss of objectivity and rigor, but rigor without commitment and vision can easily lead to rigor mortis of thought and moral energy. More to the point, it can lead to poor thinking because it separates intellect from feeling."

To this end, Meadowcreek offers a variety of educational programs. Even if you are a relative novice when it comes to environmental issues, there is a place for you at Meadowcreek as long as you are eager to learn. "The context of Meadowcreek is wonderful for reaffirming or reexamining one's beliefs," says former intern Patrick. Adds Allison, "It's a wonderful resource for anyone who would like to know more about environmental issues."

Meadowcreek's programs include three-week January terms for college students, consortia for teachers, writers, and other professionals, exchange programs, and one-day events for nature enthusiasts. But the offering that is most appropriate for recent graduates is a ten-week work/study internship, held each spring and fall. The internship is designed to introduce you to such basic environmental building blocks as sustainable agriculture, applied ecology, and renewable resource systems. Your time is divided among classroom lectures and discussions, work in the fields and greenhouses, field trips, and group projects. And each segment of your day complements the others. A morning lecture on the ramifications of global warming will become more relevant to you as you spend an afternoon in the Meadowcreek greenhouse tending to the fragile herb garden you're cultivating. "The classroom sessions are rather informal and the work sessions provided a nice complement to intellectual and philosophical explorations," says Patrick, "although the mulching of blueberry bushes came to be tedious on occasion."

The lessons you learn at the Meadowcreek internship will serve you well even if your career choice has no direct connection to environmentalism. "I walked out of there with great hope for the world," says Allison. But if you do have a related goal or you identify one during the work/study internship, you can stay on for a 27-week extended internship (or you can return for one at a later date). The extended internship allows you to dig deeper into the basic environmental issues covered in Meadowcreek's classes and discussions. Should you take it on, a Meadowcreek staff member will help you design a highly personalized independent program that relates to your specific goals. "We will sit down with you and make a specific list of what you will accomplish while you are here," says Pat, a Meadowcreek staff member. "And if we can't offer you all of the necessary experiences here, we will find places nearby where you can have those experiences."

As a Meadowcreek intern in both the work/study and the extended internship, you will live on Meadowcreek's rustic, wooded complex which includes staff houses, a conference center, farm structures, fields, and workshops. The dorms, like the other buildings, are cozy and comfortable (and environmentally sound), and you will probably have a room to yourself. You will prepare your meals along with the other interns in a communal kitchen (using many of the foods cultivated at Meadowcreek). The intern groups tend to be small—between ten and fifteen people per session. And although each group has a different chemistry, they are generally characterized by camaraderie and friendship. "You work very closely. You are colleagues, friends, classmates, everything," says Allison. Adds Patrick: "Our intern group interacted very smoothly. We shared cooking and clean-up duties and ate simple and wonderful meals together. While there was considerable philosophical alignment, there was also enough diversity that our discussions were stimulating. We also worked well together."

Beyond the world of your fellow interns, you are fully integrated into the community of Meadowcreek, a cohesive group of staff members, their spouses, and children, many of whom live on the compound, and you will meet experts from around the country who convene at Meadowcreek's annual conferences. "You start to feel like you are a part of a community of concerned people," says Sam.

While classes, discussions, and conferences will occupy most of your time, you'll find many distractions both on the property and off. The surrounding towns are rich in folk culture. The music of mandolins and banjos fill local dance-halls where clogging is the dance style of choice (many interns take clogging lessons). Meadowcreek is surrounded by a jumble of hills, mountains, and woods that are well-suited for hiking. And the nearby Buffalo River is a prime canoeing spot.

The cost of the ten-week work/study internship is $750.

That covers your housing, $25 per week worth of food, and all of your project expenses. Interns in the extended internship wind up earning money—$300 per month after you pay an initial $450 fee—but you must participate in the ten-week internship before you are eligible for the extended internship. Scholarships and financial aid are widely available.

SUMMARY

Who They Are: The Meadowcreek Project is a combination think tank, research facility, and education center that explores creative and practical solutions to environmental problems.

Where: Fox, Arkansas.

Opportunities for Recent Graduates: Although Meadowcreek offers a wide variety of educational programs, the ten-week work/study internship is most appropriate for recent graduates. Combining classroom time with work in the fields and greenhouses, the internship will introduce you to sustainable agriculture, renewable energy systems, and other building blocks of environmentalism.

Financial Arrangement: The work/study internship costs $750, which covers housing and $25 per week for food.

Time Frame: The internship is offered each spring and fall and lasts for ten weeks. If you have a specific career goal relating to environmentalism, you can stay on for an additional 27-week extended internship.

How to Apply: Contact the Meadowcreek office for an application.

Pros:

- Confronting the current environmental crisis from a hopeful, solution-oriented perspective.

- Strong sense of community.

- Teaching methods that combine the theoretical and practical.

- Previous experience in environmental science is not necessary.

Cons:

- Isolation of Fox, Arkansas.

- Small population of the community.

TEACHING SIOUX INDIAN STUDENTS

> **Red Cloud Indian School**
> Holy Rosary Mission
> Pine Ridge, South Dakota 57770
> (605) 867-5888

Few places in America are as culturally rich as the Pine Ridge Indian Reservation, a Sioux reservation in South Dakota. This is the land of Wounded Knee and Crazy Horse, and of the famed warrior Red Cloud, for whom the Red Cloud Indian School, a Jesuit School on the reservation, is named.

But at the same time, few places have been harder hit by poverty. The reservation is the poorest in the county in the United States, with unemployment hovering at 80 percent and alcoholism and teen pregnancy endemic. "The problems of the Indians are the problems of poor people everywhere," says Sean, a recent Notre Dame graduate and Red Cloud Volunteer. "They're not more romantic because they're Indians."

Part of the mission of the Red Cloud Indian School, the country's largest private school for native American children, is helping its Sioux students lift themselves out of the cycle of poverty without leaving behind their Indian heritage and values. "The families are very strong and supportive here," says Father David Matzko, the superintendent of Red Cloud. "Leaving the reservation is very hard. When they go away, they become a minority. Life is hard here, but at least they're not disciminated against."

The school, which was founded a hundred years ago at the request of Red Cloud himself, teaches a traditional curriculum peppered with courses on Indian heritage and Lakota language (the native Sioux language which many of the students speak among themselves). "We're very demanding," says Father Matzko. "We want to teach them that they have the ability to achieve if they want to."

Volunteers work with the staff of native Americans, Jesuit priests and nuns, and they usually hold down several jobs at once. They work as teachers (elective courses only, unless you're certified), sports coaches, bus drivers, tutors, office and maintenance workers. Tamara, a recent graduate of Kenyon College, taught an elective course in child psychology, drove a bus, and coached Red Cloud's cheerleading squad. Sean taught physics, photography, and an astronomy elective.

Given its location on the edge of a vast but remote Indian reservation ninety miles from the nearest city (Rapid City), Red Cloud can't offer much in the way of structured diversions. "It's a very peaceful, quiet place," says Tamara. "And you do need some ability to be on your own."

And while the isolation can be nerve-racking, especially in the winter when travel is difficult ("You can get a little stir-crazy"), volunteers seem to have little trouble filling up their days. Most teach classes every day, and supervise extracurricular activities, such as sports, clubs or workshops in the afternoon and evenings. "I would have class until 3:00, and either work in the darkroom or take a bike ride in the afternoon," says Sean. "After dinner, I would grade labs and papers or take the kids to the school's telescope, which is one of the best in South Dakota. I taught myself how to use it and we would spend a lot of time looking at stars." During the sports seasons, there are games nearly every night, including bus rides of up to ninety miles to reach opponents in Montana and North Dakota. "The social life revolves around the school," says Sean.

The remoteness of the school tends to promote strong friendships among volunteers, staff and students. "There's a lot of hanging-out going on," says Sean. Volunteers live together, women in one house ("a cozy, ramshackle log cabin called the cottage"), men in another ("It's not as nice as the cottage, so we call it the chateau to make it sound nicer"). Students are forthcoming with invitations to the reservation. "The best reward is getting to know the kids," says Sean. "And there's a lot they can show you, even if it's just hunting or digging wild turnips—that you can take away with you."

The cultural riches on the reservation are generally open to volunteers. "They welcome you if you're there for the right reasons." says Sean. "I went to some powwows, where there was a lot of dancing and disorganized fun. Other volunteers go to the sweat lodge, a little igloo-shaped building made of branches and covered with cloth and filled with hot rocks. It's a sauna where the native Americans smoke a pipe as a mode of prayer. They don't want anthropologists coming, but if you just want to get involved, there's a lot available for you."

Volunteers at Red Cloud don't need any special experience or expertise, although any teaching experience is an obvious boost. What is important, though, is a basic sensitivity to the cultural and social uniqueness of kids growing up on an Indian reservation. "These kids have seen more of life at an earlier age than most of their peers elsewhere," says Father Matzko. Adds Sean: "A lot of the students have kids of their own; some have a couple of kids. Absenteeism [in the classroom] is a horrible problem here. But if a student has a sick baby that has to go to the hospital, what is more important?"

SUMMARY

What They Do: The Red Cloud School, a Catholic school, is the largest private school for Indians in the country.

Where: Pine Ridge, South Dakota (two hours from Rapid City).

Opportunities for Recent Graduates: Volunteers are tutors and coaches, bus drivers, and office workers. Those who are certified teach regular classes.

Financial Arrangement: Room and board plus a stipend of $125 per month.

Time Frame: Most volunteers commit for one or two years.

Number of Positions: Up to thirteen.

How to Apply: Most volunteers begin in August, at the beginning of the school year. Contact Father David Matzko, superintendent.

Pros:

- Close friendships with students.

- Learning about Indian culture.

- Getting serious work experience.

Cons:

• Isolation.

• Poverty on the reservation.

WORKING WITH CHILDREN

St. Jude's Ranch for Children
100 St. Jude's Street
P.O. Box 985
Boulder City, Nevada 89005-0985
(702) 293-3131

St. Jude's Ranch is a refuge for physically and emotionally abused children and adolescents. Set against the dusty
landscape of the Mojave Desert—an unlikely setting for
such a fertile institution—its small complex of low-rise
buildings is home to thirty-nine children at a time. The
children (as young as six years old) come from family situations ranging from disruptive to deadly. Many of them
stay until they're adults.
St. Jude's (it's not a real ranch) offers its children
warmth and support in an atmosphere that manages to be
both cozy and disciplined. Pet dogs and cats roam the
grounds and skateboards are an accepted mode of transportation. Each child is part of a "cottage family"—eight chil-

dren and two adults living together. Though St. Jude's as a whole is a fairly close-knit community, this smaller family group provides the real nurturing for the children. It's the cottage parents who go to teacher conferences (St. Jude's children attend public school), coach Little League teams, sit through dance recitals, and nag about unmade beds. "The cottage parent's job is to try to make a normal life for the children," says Carl, a St. Jude's volunteer.

Volunteers fit in as an added tier of support for the children, cottage parents, and ranch staff. It's the volunteers who keep the ranch library organized and staffed, the snack bar running, and the property maintained. But they also have the opportunity to work closely with the children. Volunteers often step in when house parents are on vacation, working as tutors, coaches, and often simply companions. The ranch staff also encourages volunteers to share any interests or skills they have with the children, such as music, drama, or photography. "The house parents are like real parents, and they have to be disciplinarians," says Carl. "We're not in that role and we have a chance to be more like friends with the children. It's a more comfortable relationship."

St. Jude's offers a generous benefits package—room, board, and a $200 per month stipend. Though some volunteers stay for years at a time, the greatest opportunity for young people is probably over the summer, when the children are not in school. Positions may be hard to come by and applications should be filled out as far in advance as possible.

SUMMARY

Who They Are: St. Jude's Ranch for Children is a home for physically and emotionally abused children and adolescents.

Where: Boulder City, Nevada (twenty miles from Las Vegas).

Opportunities for Recent Graduates: Volunteers help the ranch staff with administrative and maintenance work and work directly with the children as tutors, teachers, and coaches.

Financial Arrangement: Volunteers receive room and board (private, dorm-style room), plus $200 a month.

Time Frame: Flexible, with most volunteers serving from three months to one year.

Number of Positions: Approximately eight.

How to Apply: There is no formal deadline or starting date, but positions are scarce, so applications should be filed as far in advance as is possible. Contact St. Jude's for more information.

Pros:

- Family atmosphere.

- Opportunity to work closely with children.

Cons:

- Isolation.

- Few volunteer positions.

A VOLUNTEER PLACEMENT PROGRAM

```
VISTA
806 Connecticut Avenue, NW
Washington, D.C. 20525
(800) 424-8867
```

Contrary to popular belief, VISTA is alive and well. It did not, as most people seem to believe, vanish with the era that spawned it, the sixties. Though it has suffered major budget cuts in the past couple of decades, it still exists today, albeit rather quietly. And most surprising, it's something of a gem.

VISTA (Volunteers in Service to America) is a full-time volunteer program for Americans 18 and older. It falls under the umbrella of ACTION, the agency that coordinates most U.S. government-run volunteer organizations. Any U.S. citizen is eligible, providing he or she is at least 18, has no serious medical problems or sordid criminal record, and is willing to commit for one year. Volunteers work with non-profit agencies throughout the United States.

The benefits are downright lavish. The U.S. government pays all VISTA volunteers a monthly salary of just over $500. Blue Cross and Blue Shield coverage is included, life insurance is available—inexpensively—for those in the market, and at the end of your term, you receive as a readjustment allowance $75 for each month you've served.

What's more, VISTA is, generally, easy to join. All volunteer placements are handled through 53 regional offices. You contact the office in the area you would like to serve and they send you a list of local non-profit agencies that are accredited VISTA sponsors. All of the agencies deal with the poor and disadvantaged. The list of New York VISTA projects, for instance, includes thirty-three agencies, such as Parents Anonymous, Literacy Volunteers of New York City, New York State Coalition Against Domestic Violence, and the International Center for the Disabled. It's up to you to contact the agencies that appeal to you and set up interviews, inasmuch as the agencies do their own hiring, independent of the VISTA office.

As a VISTA volunteer, you become a full-time staff member of agencies such as Vermont's Committee on Temporary Shelter, Louisiana's Greater Baton Rouge Food Bank, and the Women's Service Center in Pittsfield, Massachusetts. These agencies, for the most part, are underfunded and understaffed. VISTA volunteers should expect to fill positions of substance. In the Boston office of the Massachusetts Association of Older Americans, for instance, VISTA volunteers are out in the field helping elderly individuals take full advantage of the range of services available to them. At the Berkshire Training and Employment Program, it's a VISTA volunteer who heads up the agency's recruitment program, traveling from school to school in Berkshire country to track down disadvantaged students who could benefit from the agency's programs. There is no real uniformity in the positions offered within each sponsoring agency, so you should get a clear job description before you commit.

There aren't many recent graduates within the ranks of VISTA, but there is a small contingent. For the most part, VISTA volunteers include many retirees, housewives, and welfare recipients who are aware that they can supplement their income through VISTA without jeopardizing their welfare payments. Otherwise, VISTA has trouble recruiting volunteers, especially on the east and west coasts. This is not a reflection of the quality of the program; rather, as many state officers agree, it's a result of poor publicity. "We are doing little national recruitment," says Diana London from VISTA's Washington Headquarters. "It's up to the states to recruit their own people." Many states make the mistake of promoting VISTA positions as job opportunities rather than volunteer experiences. The VISTA salary and benefits are generous by volunteer standards, but they're inadequate for anyone with serious financial responsibilities. "We actually lose people to McDonald's," says one regional officer.

Of course, this just leaves more room for recent graduates, well-accustomed to shoestring living and looking for a challenging volunteer experience. For this body of volunteers, VISTA service is well worth pursuing.

SUMMARY

Who They Are: Volunteers in Service to America (VISTA) is a domestic volunteer placement program funded by the United States government.

Where: VISTA volunteers serve in all fifty states, plus Washington D.C., Puerto Rico, and the Virgin Islands.

Opportunities for Recent Graduates: Volunteers work for a wide variety of non-profit agencies.

Financial Arrangement: Volunteers receive a stipend of approximately $500 per month, paid for by the U.S. government. In addition, upon completion of service, volunteers are paid a readjustment allowance of $75 for each month served.

Time Frame: One-year minimum.

Number of Positions: Appoximately 2,600.

How to Apply: Contact the Washington office for the telephone number of the state office closest to the area you'd like to serve. The state office will provide you with a list of approved sponsoring agencies, which you then contact directly. Volunteers are hired by the sponsoring agency, independent from VISTA. On the average, volunteers begin working within two to three months of their first contact with the state office.

Pros:

- Varied job options.

- Regular, forty-hour work week.

- Generous benefits paid by the government.

Cons:

- Difficult to switch jobs in mid-program.

- Working with state and federal bureaucracies.

CHRISTIAN ORGANIZATIONS

The following volunteer placement organizations are open only to Christians. You don't have to be a devout

Christian but, as one program director puts it, you do "at least have to be in a dialogue with Christianity." Although these organizations may not be appropriate for many graduates, they have played an enormous role in the development of volunteerism in this country and around the world. They also offer some top-notch opportunities.

- **Brethren Volunteer Service**
  1451 Dundee Avenue
  Elgin, Illinois 60120
  (312) 742-5100

- **Jesuit Volunteer Corps (Northwest)**
  P.O. Box 3928
  Portland, OR 97208
  (503) 228-2457

- **Jesuit Volunteer Corps (East)**
  Eighteenth and Thompson Streets
  Philadelphia, PA 19121
  (215) 232-0300

- **Jesuit Volunteer Corps (Midwest)**
  P.O. Box 32692
  Detroit, MI 48232
  (313) 894-1140

- **Jesuit Volunteer Corps (Southwest)**
  1427 12th Street
  Oakland, CA 94607
  (415) 465-5016

- **Jesuit Volunteer Corps (South)**
  1505 Kane Street
  Houston, TX 77007
  (713) 223-5387

- **Lutheran Volunteer Corps**
  1333 N Street, NW
  Washington, D.C. 20005
  (202) 387-3222

- **Mennonite Voluntary Service**
  Box 347
  Newton, Kansas 67114-0347
  316-283-5100

RECOMMENDED READING

Volunteer!: The Comprehensive guide to voluntary service in the U.S. and abroad. This book, written by Marjorie Cohen in collaboration with the Council on International Educational Exchange, is the Michelin Guide to voluntary experience all over the world. The single-space format is slightly off-putting and the listings stick to the basics, but it's crammed with information, and for a truly complete guide to voluntary service, it's unbeatable ($4.95, Council on International Educational Exchange, 205 East 42nd Street, New York, New York, 10017; (212) 661-1414).

Alternatives to the Peace Corps: Gaining Third World Experience. Published by the Institute for Food and Development Policy, this no-frills pamphlet is accessible and well-structured. It includes most of the major volunteer organizations and some good general information about volunteering ($3.00, Institute for Food and Development Policy, 145 Ninth Street, San Francisco, California 94103; (415) 864-8555).

Connections: This pamphlet, distributed free, is geared toward Christians, although it also includes some secular organizations. It's published by the *St. Vincent Pallotti Center for Apostolic Development* (715 Monroe Street, NE, Washington, D.C. 20017-1755; (202) 529-3330).

The Overseas List: This well-written, carefully researched book is for Christian professionals and volunteers seeking work in developing countries. In addition to its exhaustive listing of resources, this book offers valuble advice and wisdom from its three experienced authors ($12.95, Augsburg Publishing House, 426 South Fifth Street, Box 1209, Minneapolis, Minnesota 55440; (612) 330-3456).

Intercristo: A Seattle-based information center, Intercristo maintains a file of thousands of volunteer and job positions among over four hundred Christian mission agencies. For a small fee ($35 in 1988), they'll run a profile of your skills, interests, and motivations through their computer and give you back a list of work possibilities (P.O. Box 33487, Seattle, WA 98133; (206) 546-7330).

The Response: Though it covers much of the same territory as *Connections, The Response* is one of the best known and most concise volunteer resources extant. It's available free from *International Liaison of Lay Volunteers in Mission* (4121 Harewood Road, N.E., P.O. Box 29149, Washington, D.C. 20017-9149; (202) 529-1100).

SEEDS Magazine, "Volunteer! What You Need to Know about 23 Organizations." A widely distributed reprint of an article from the Christian magazine SEEDS, This is a straightforward guide to the world's major development organizations, including those soliciting volunteers ($2.50, SEEDS Resources, 222 East Lake Drive, Decatur, Georgia, 30030).

OPPORTUNITIES IN THE OUTDOORS

CHAPTER THREE

Between America's teeming cities and strips of highway is a vast trove of natural treasures. America's wilderness—from sun-roasted deserts and raging rivers to cool and silent forests and lumbering mountains—is more varied than any other on earth. And it contains an endless array of wonderful opportunities.

Thousands of people, most of them young and many of them just out of college, parlay their love for the outdoors into some outstanding experiences in America's parks, forests, national seashores, and wilderness areas. They study moose populations in Alaska and rare birds in Hawaii, greet campers in Yellowstone National Park, lead cave tours in Texas, and canyon tours in Arizona. They study ancient skeletons in Utah and blaze trails along the Oregon coast.

The prime sources of these and other opportunities in the outdoors are the agencies—public and private—that manage America's open land. It takes an enormous amount of manpower to keep the country's parks in top shape for recreation, research, and resource development. There are thousands of miles of trails to be maintained, hundreds of campgrounds to be staffed, millions of years of natural history to be explained, and scores of plants, animals and minerals to be studied. The guardians of America's wilderness —the United States Forest Service, the National Park Service, the Bureau of Land Management, and other federal, state and private wildlife agencies—simply can't afford to pay full-fledged, full-time staffers to do it all.

So in many cases, these agencies will gladly pay your room, board, and basic expenses in exchange for your help patrolling mountain ranges, counting falcons, photographing archaeological ruins, or whatever else needs to be done. You won't earn a conventional salary. And in many cases the work is taxing. But you'll be living in some of the most glorious settings of the world, like Glacier National Park in Montana, Acadia National Park in Maine, the Grand Canyon in Arizona, Alaska's mountain ranges, and Hawaii's rugged rain forests. You can get hands-on experience in a range of disciplines, including wildlife research, resource management, conservation, and recreation. "If you just want to see another part of the country, it's a great thing to do," says Molly, a journalism major from the University of Wisconsin who worked as an assistant campground ranger at Maine's Baxter State Park. "If you want to explore career opportunities, it's a great thing to do. If you want to explore some personal issues, it's a great thing to do. And if you want to combine career and personal things, it's a great thing to do."

VOLUNTEERS IN THE PARK (VIP)

There are thousands of expense-paying volunteer positions in the parks, forests, and wilderness areas around

America. These positions, known by some agency officials as Volunteer in the Park positions (VIP), are not the same as seasonal jobs. As a VIP, you'll be working alongside seasonal workers, often in the same job. As a VIP, however, you will receive only room, board, and some pocket change, whereas your seasonal-worker colleagues will be paid a conventional salary. In addition, seasonal jobs are extremely competitive and typically reserved for people committed to a career with one of the agencies. Conversely, VIP positions are easier to come by, with housing being the main limiting factor at most parks.

Whether you're a graduate of wilderness survival camp or a lifelong city dweller, there is a VIP position out there for you. If you love to deal with people, you could be a campground host and spend your days talking to campers from all over the world. If you're crowd-weary from dormitory life, you could become a back-country ranger and spend weeks roaming the wilderness on your own. Archaeology majors can help catalog the artifacts and remains of an ancient tribe of native American Indians that died off in the seventh century. Potential professors can lecture on the wildlife of the desert. And computer majors can set up programs for keeping track of plant species.

These and countless other positions abound. But you have to know where to look. Blindly winding through the labyrinth of federal, state, and regional offices trying to find an expense-paid volunteer position can be exasperating. There is absolutely no central coordination between the different agencies and little between the separate parks and forests. There are well over one thousand recreation and wilderness areas in this country, and each hires its own staff based on its own needs, budget, and housing capacity. Using the information provided in this chapter, however, you'll have no trouble tracking down a position.

LIFE AS A VOLUNTEER

First, there are some things you should know about life as a VIP. Living and working in the outdoors is more than a steady job and a backyard full of natural masterpieces. And you don't have to forgo all of the comforts of home (unless you want to). Neither do you have to live like a hermit.

Most important, volunteers and agency staff members agree, is taking stock of your needs before you start thinking about a position and location. "Many people come here out of the urban areas and their dream is to be a cowboy, to work outdoors," says John Bustos, a wildlife biologist and human resource coordinator for the forest service in Colorado. "What really matters is that they think about what they want to do and why they're doing it before they arrive. Sometimes, your real dreams don't take your real life values into account." In other words, a gorgeous sunrise and the howl of coyotes won't take the place of a comfortable bed, if that is something very dear to you. And with such a huge variety of locations and jobs to choose from, you can afford to hold out for a position that really suits you.

What you eat, where you sleep and shower, how you have fun—every aspect of your life—is dictated by the kind of job and location you choose. And each combination of job and location translates into a different quality of life. If you're a wildlife researcher working in the lab on the edge of the park, you might live with other volunteers in a spacious apartment or motel suite. Campground hosts, rangers and maintenance workers often live in well-appointed cabins and trailers, while others live in tents that they bring from home. "Whatever the case, you don't go into the area blind," says volunteer Molly. "Your supervisor will tell you what to expect. I lived in a cabin, a true cabin, with no running water or outlets, on a beautiful, clean pond where I swam every morning. And if I wanted to shower, I went to one of the ranger's houses."

Your food allowance will keep your belly full, but don't expect to be shaving truffles onto your macaroni and cheese. A typical weekly food stipend is $40, although that can double if you're in a pricey area, like Alaska or Hawaii. You will probably be responsible for buying your own food and cooking it yourself in the kitchen of your apartment or cabin, on a campground grill, or your own portable gas stove. "We all get together for dinner a few nights a week," says Mike, a recent graduate who worked in Hawaii's Haleakala National Park. "That cuts down on the work and the cost, and it's fun."

Sometimes getting to the food is more problematic than affording it. "I have to drive ten miles just to get a quart of milk," says Hugh, a Columbia College graduate working in Oregon's Alsea Falls Recreation Site. "And since I don't have a car, I have to ride my bike or sleaze off someone who has a car."

Transportation woes are common among volunteers, most of whom are without cars. But nobody I spoke to had serious complaints. "You shouldn't come here expecting to be a social butterfly," says Hugh. "But there's enough to keep busy." Adds Mike of Hawaii: "We spend a lot of time trying to figure out how to get off the mountain. We're an hour from the coast and two hours from the center of tourism. So whenever we know of someone going down, we tend to grab the chance. But we really enjoy the place where we're living. We hike into the crater, and we live across from a grove of exotic trees."

Socially speaking, life on the banks of a volcanic crater or in a remote wildlife refuge isn't frat row at Ole Miss. But again, some places are more active than others, and in talking to potential supervisors, you'll be able to take the pulse before you commit. Some people actually seem to flourish.

"I dated a ranger," says Molly, "which is more common than you'd think. Most of them are right out of school. And I did things with other volunteers, like playing horseshoes, drinking beers, having campfires, and talking, the same things you'd do with your friends from home." For people in some of the larger, more popular parks, in fact, making close friends is easy compared to finding time to be alone. "My campground hosts are always amazed at the new network of friends they come away with," says Doug Caldwell, the regional director of the National Park Service's Rocky Mountain office.

In many of the smaller parks, however, your only social prospects might be in a nearby town. "There are only four of us working here," says Hugh. "But I get into town, and the people are really friendly. They don't blink as much when they're talking as the people in New York."

As an expense-paid volunteer, all of your basic needs are accounted for, and money (or lack of it) shouldn't produce great stress. There certainly are not many material temptations. But volunteers agree that you should bring along a few hundred dollars in spending money ("I worked at a temp job before I started," says Molly), as there will be opportunities to leave the park on days off. And even camping trips cost a few dollars. "The forty dollars they give me every week covered my basic needs," says Molly. "It didn't cover a beer and a movie. And it would have been a shame not to have been able to explore."

THE JOBS

Here are some general descriptions of the positions most commonly advertised in the parks, forests, and wilderness areas around the country. The setting will have a huge impact on the reality of each position (see page 175 for more information), but the basic parameters and responsibilities are pretty consistent.

CAMPGROUND HOST/ RECREATION AIDE

Campground host is perhaps the most popular position among expense-paid volunteers, and it has a lot to offer someone right out of college. It's a social position, putting you in contact with people of all ages, from all over the world, from all different backgrounds, and it requires little or no training. Since nearly every recreation area uses campground hosts, the positions are, in general, easy to come by if you get your name in early in the year (start looking around December).

As a campground host, you will live among the campers at the campground. You are officially the liaison between the campers and the rangers, but what you really do is make the campers feel at home at the campsite. You make sure they know about the park's rules, services, sights, and activities. You help them pitch their tent or hook up their RV. You tell them where they can hike, when they can shower, and why they shouldn't keep their leftover grilled salmon near the entrance of their tent (bear bait). And you are the first person campers will turn to if any problems come up, from a blasting radio or a broken shower to a medical emergency.

The main requirement for being a campground host is enjoying people. "You try to help people whenever you can," says one forest service agent. "They want to know where they can get firewood, where they put their child, where they can take a strenuous hike, where they can buy a map, where they can see eagles. And you keep answering them."

Other responsibilities vary from park to park. Many

hosts, in addition to mingling with the campers, are in charge of keeping the place in good physical shape. "I learned to put new roofs on the lean-tos," says Molly. "I would make sure the flag was up, that the weather forecast had been logged, which is important when people are hiking way up into the mountains. I also did some unappealing jobs like cleaning. But I spent most of my time talking to the public, which I really enjoyed. I was the authority figure there. And I met some great people." When you're comparing the merits of different campgrounds, get a plain description of all of the maintenance duties you will have. Some hosts don't lift a finger. Others, though, are charged with such baneful tasks as cleaning outhouses. ("It's not as bad as it sounds," says Hugh. "If you can stomach the *thought* of doing it, you can stomach *actually* doing it.")

Although campground hosts always live among the campers, the details of the housing arrangement vary from park to park. In some cases, you will have your own cabin or trailer in a location that's accessible to the campground guests. In others, you will be asked to bring your own camping equipment and pitch a tent like everyone else, though you'll usually have your pick of the best campsites.

Your work schedule, too, will depend on where you are. The best arrangement has hosts working for four and a half to five days at a stretch with two days off in a row. During the time you're on duty, you're technically on call 24 hours a day, and should never stray far from your outpost. But during your time off, you roam free.

SUMMARY

Responsibilities: Hosts help campers get settled and informed about park rules and attractions. They handle small problems that come up, and often have to participate in the maintenance of the facilities.

Requirements: You must enjoy being around people and be naturally helpful, outgoing, and upbeat.

Financial Arrangement: All campground host positions include either housing or a choice campsite. Stipends vary from park to park, and some are rather tight-fisted. But the average is $40 per week.

Pros:

- Making friends from all over the country.

- Being in a position of authority.

- Positions are fairly easy to get without previous experience.

Cons:

- Little privacy.

- Possibility of cleaning outhouses and other odious maintenance tasks.

INTERPRETATION/
EDUCATIONAL AIDE

Educating the public about the natural history, human history, and scenic value of an area has always been a priority within the different land management agencies. "We're always trying to get our constituency involved with what we're doing," says Penelope Faulkner, a forest service agent in Washington state. At the most rudimentary level, "interpretation" is the pamphlet handed out at the visitor's center at Carlsbad Cavern illustrating how sediments of an ancient sea formed the area's unique landscape.

But in many parks, historic sites, and wilderness areas, interpretation and education is an elaborate sideshow to the area's natural wonders. It often involves teams of trained staff members, high-budget films, and not-quite-Broadway-caliber live history shows in which employees dress up and act out, for instance, the domestic life of George Washington. At such levels, being an interpretation aide calls for some creativity.

Volunteers lead trail tours, nature, wildlife, and botany tours, narrate slide shows, and lead other educational forums. And while some of the subjects can be on the esoteric side—such as four billion years of the earth's development embodied in a canyon wall—you don't usually need a background in what you're teaching.

Rather, you need the same qualities that make for a good campground host: a basic enjoyment of people and the ability to project a pleasant, helpful attitude (despite whining children and blatantly bored tourists). "I was giving history and natural history talks and telling people why this area is so special," says Mike, a volunteer at Hawaii's Haleakala National Park. "But what I most enjoyed was interacting with people afterwards. They really seemed to have a big interest in it. I was able to feel the pulse of what the public was thinking environmentally. Eighty percent of the people really had a strong feeling that something needs to be done environmentally. The other 20 percent were simply uninformed and wanted to learn more."

While some programs are tightly formatted, many leave room for your own style. On a recent trip to the U.S.S. *Arizona* Memorial at Pearl Harbor, for instance, I had an interpretation guide who read sections of letters of servicemen who lost their lives in the Japanese attack. This very moving closing to an otherwise prosaic presentation was her own touch.

Most interpretation jobs include some behind-the-desk time, and in some places answering questions and handing out pamphlets balances out the more demanding, performance-like tours. Just make sure the balance is acceptable to you before you commit to the position.

SUMMARY

Responsibilities: Interpretation aides help educate the public about an area's historic, natural, and scenic wonders. They lead nature hikes and narrate slide shows, give history lectures and guided tours, and dispense written material.

Requirements: You should be naturally upbeat and patient, enjoy answering questions, and be comfortable addressing large groups.

Financial Arrangement: Accommodations for interpretation aides vary from park to park, but typically you'll live on the camping premises in a dorm-style arrangement with other volunteers and seasonal staff members. Stipends also vary, but the average pay is $40 per week.

Pros:

- Plenty of social interaction.

- The chance to enlighten people about significant environmental issues.

- Flexibility for personal style.

Cons:

- Boredom behind an information desk.

- Disinterested tourists.

MAINTENANCE AIDE

There's little glamour in clearing trails, fixing picnic tables, or painting cabins. But for some people, a maintenance job is an ideal, low-pressure way to stay in shape and enjoy the wilderness. "I really didn't care what I was doing, I just wanted to be outdoors," says Hugh, who's doing maintenance at Oregon's Alsea Falls Recreation Site. "Every day, you have your own specific job. It's very task-oriented and I find it's a good change of pace, a respite between graduation and career. You can really get your mind straight."

Volunteers and agency staff warn that straight maintenance work, eight hours a day, can lead to quick burnout, so you should look for a position that is peppered with some learning opportunities. "I'm squeezing a lot of people for information," says Hugh, "and they've been giving me some bonuses. I'm exposed to timber sales and timber cruising. They sent me out with the botanists and fisheries people. So I've been learning."

SUMMARY

Responsibilities: Maintenance volunteers clear trails, clean campgrounds, paint facilities, chop wood, and perform other tasks relating to the physical upkeep of the area.

Requirements: Maintenance volunteers should be in good physical condition and be willing to work hard.

Financial Arrangement: Accommodations vary from park to park, but you will usually live in a dorm-style arrangement with other volunteers and seasonal workers. Stipends also vary, but your bargaining power increases as the labor gets more strenuous. An average stipend is $40 per week.

Pros:

- Low-pressure work environment.

- Getting into shape through physical labor.

Cons:

- Unavoidable, undesirable tasks, like cleaning outhouses.

- Burnout potential.

RANGER

A well-rounded ranger position is the plum volunteer job. But each park has its own definition of a volunteer ranger, so be sure to clarify the responsibilities before you commit. The two positions listed below are those most commonly offered.

BACK-COUNTRY RANGER

Back-country ranger positions, perhaps the most romantic of the outdoor opportunities, are for solitary souls with rugged appetites. With the bare necessities strapped across their shoulders, back-country rangers take to the wilderness by themselves, often for weeks at a time. They roam the most remote stretches of the parks, watching for campers and hikers who might need assistance, for wounded animals, blocked trails, and scourges like illegal campfires and heavy-handed campers.

"For me it was a time to relax," says Molly, who hit the back country for a week while at Maine's Baxter State Park. "It was spiritually satisfying to be out there alone, doing my own writing, being a part of the wilderness rather than just working in the wilderness."

Depending on the terrain, back-country rangers come from different levels of experience. In the remote outer reaches of Alaska, where a back-country ranger might wander for a month and not see a trace of human activity, solid experience (beyond a few family camping trips) in the outdoors is a must. You should feel confident of coping both physically and mentally, with such problems as snakebites, sprained ankles, and wrong turns.

But in other parks, where back-country areas are smaller,

tamer, and more populated, the staff might unleash you as long as you have basic camping and hiking skills.

SUMMARY

Responsibilities: Back-country rangers patrol remote wilderness areas, making sure that campers and hikers are safe and obeying the rules.

Requirements: You should be a clear thinker with the ability to be absolutely alone for extended periods, and you should have extensive experience in the outdoors.

Financial Arrangement: Back-country ranagers usually provide their own camping equipment and receive a small weekly food stipend. When not in the back country, back-country ranger accommodations vary from park to park, but you will probably be put up in the dorm-style housing of the other volunteers and seasonal workers. Average stipend is $40 per week.

Pros:

- Allows you to spend time in unspoiled wilderness areas.

- Fosters self-reliance.

Cons:

- Inevitable bouts of loneliness.

- A moderate risk factor.

RANGER/ASSISTANT RANGER

The more general ranger or assistant ranger positions will keep you closer to base camp. These positions are most notable for their jack-of-all-trades quality. And the best positions offer you a taste of many different facets of the park. You might spend a week issuing back-country permits or offering hiking directions and warnings about "beaver fever," the stomach affliction often caused by drinking untreated water from streams. Or you might be assigned to lead trail tours, staff information desks, and asked to help out an emergency trail-repair crew. "It's a good way to see where you fit in best," says Jim Eicher, an agency outdoor recreation planner in California.

Not all of the assistant ranger positions are equally flexible. So before you sign on, make sure you won't be relegated to just one post. "I know people who spent their whole time collecting fees in the ticket booth," says one volunteer. "They didn't really mind it, but I'd go crazy."

SUMMARY

Responsibilities: Assistant rangers are jack-of-all-trades, helping out in interpretation, maintenance, and recreation as they're needed.

Requirements: You should be a team-spirited type with the flexibility to move from job to job, and you should enjoy dealing with people.

Financial Arrangement: Accommodations vary from park to park, with most rangers living in dorm-style accommodations with other volunteers and seasonal workers. Average stipend is $40.

Pros:

- Learning about different facets of park management.

- Balance of group and solo work.

- Plenty of social opportunity.

Cons:

- Intermittent mundane job assignments.

- Missing out on an in-depth job experience.

WILDLIFE RESEARCH ASSISTANT

As condo parks and parking lots devour the open spaces of America, wilderness preserves are increasingly vulnerable to human activity. One manifestation of this problem is currently being studied in the wilderness areas outside San Francisco. It seems that zealous development in the previously untouched areas around the borders of the park has driven large populations of bobcats and coyotes into the preserve. As these predatory animals scour the preserve for new food sources, deer and other animals these animals prey upon are in danger.

Monitoring the population of predatory animals and

their prey near San Francisco is one of hundreds of ecological issues currently being addressed in the wilderness areas around the country. In an age of frenetic development, crowding, and pollution, maintaining the often precarious natural balance in wilderness areas around the country requires ongoing efforts by scores of research specialists. And they often need some help.

"There are times when you simply need a second pair of eyes and hands to go out with the naturalist and do surveys on plants, or a count of animals," says Doug Caldwell, regional director of the National Park Service's Rocky Mountain office. "At Yellowstone, they might be involved with studying the elk population or water fowl. At Mesa Verde, it might be the health of mule deer."

Depending on where in the country they are, wildlife research assistants are participating in field and lab studies of endangered species, like the bald eagle, and threatened species, like the spotted owl. They study the habitats of these animals, track down nesting and calving areas, and maintain accurate counts. "I work from 1 P.M. to midnight," says Marcia, a Kenyon College graduate working in Oregon with the Bureau of Land Management. "On an average day, I go out into the wilderness to the spotted owl sights. We call the owls and see if they respond. We see if they're nesting, and do a lot of banding, which I'm just learning to do. It's really interesting work and I'm getting hands-on experience."

Wildlife research assistants, in general, are considering a career in a related field, and often have to show evidence of a serious interest, such as a major field of study in college. Some organizations, however, hire people who are simply eager to learn.

The accommodations for research assistants tend to be less rustic than those for campground hosts. "We live in apartments that are about a mile from work," says Marcia. "They're really nice two-bedroom apartments." But again, it varies, site by site. "In some cases, we rent motel rooms for the assistants," says Ray Naddy, Marcia's supervisor at the BLM office in Oregon. "For our people in the boonies, we have camper trailers."

SUMMARY

Responsibilities: Wildlife research assistants work with wildlife specialists on field and lab studies of animals and their habitats.

Requirements: Many positions require previous experience or college-level course work, plus an intent to pursue the field.

Financial Arrangement: Researchers frequently live in more populated areas of the park land, or with other volunteers and seasonal staff members in dorm-style housing. An average weekly stipend is $40.

Pros:

- Gaining practical field experience.

- Learning about animals and their habitats.

Cons:

- Some positions are subject to stringent academic or practical requirements.

OTHER OPTIONS

"We need more than just strong backs to help clear trails," says Roy Graybill, the National Park Service's national VIP coordinator. "Think about any special talents you have. You'd be surprised how many diferent kinds of people we can use."

Many of the projects under way at the parks around the country call for the kind of special talent that doesn't fit into the average park budget. So if you have a skill or are interested in developing a burgeoning talent, like writing, photography, archaeology, or computers, you could barter your services for room and board. You'll still be living close to nature. But you'll be expanding your mind, and, potentially, your resume.

You might, for instance, nurture your college newspaper-born writing skills by coming up with snappy copy for pamphlets that tells visitors at South Dakota's Wind Cave National Park the story of how the surrounding Black Hills were taken from the Sioux Indians after gold was discovered. If you're worried about plumping up your graphic art portfolio, you could offer to redesign the recreation opportunity guide at Idaho's Payette National Forest. You could seal your computer programming resume by creating a program to help a state park keep track of its expanding inventory of exotic plants. Or you could boost your chances for a job in some publication's photography department by organizing and cataloging the vast collection of nineteenth-century photographs at Mesa Verde National Park.

FINDING AN EXPENSE-PAID VOLUNTEER POSITION

There are three ways to get yourself an expense-paid volunteer position, all explained below. The first method, which is also the easiest, is to put yourself into the hands of the **Student Conservation Association,** a nonprofit agency that specializes in placing students and other adults in expense-paid volunteer positions outdoors. The second method is more laborious, but also more thorough. It involves sending away for a copy of *Helping Out in the Outdoors,* a no-frills catalog of volunteer opportunities in the wilderness, and investigating job openings on your own. The third method, for those who know exactly where they want to work, is simply to call that park headquarters directly and talk to the volunteer coordinator. This is particularly effective when dealing with the big National Parks, like Glacier, Yosemite, and Grand Canyon, which don't often list their volunteer openings with the SCA or in *Helping Out in the Outdoors.* So the only way to find out about opportunities in these locations is to call the parks on your own.

All three methods are perfectly sound, so you should choose the one that fits your style of getting things done. If you were the kind of college student who wouldn't sign up for a course until you interviewed the professor and the TA and sat through two weeks of lectures, you might enjoy taking matters into your own hands and working with *Helping Out in the Oudoors.* Less methodical types will be better off with the Student Conservation Association. And those who have always dreamed of working at Yellowstone should just pick up the phone.

METHOD 1

The **Student Conservation Association**
P.O. Box 550-C
Charlestown, New Hampshire 03603
(603) 826-5206/5741

The Student Conservation Association has been placing students and adults in expense-paying volunteer jobs and internships in the outdoors since 1957. It is held in high esteem by both the land management agencies that rely on SCA volunteers and the volunteers themselves.

As an SCA volunteer or "resource associate," you work in the same capacity as VIPs and other volunteers—as a recreation aide or a back-country ranger, an interpretation aide or a campground host. In most cases, you're working alongside other volunteers. "The only real difference I see in SCAs and other volunteers is that SCAs have their transportation to the site paid for, and regular volunteers don't," says Mike, a volunteer at Haleakala Crater in Hawaii.

But working with SCA has some real advantages that go beyond transportation (although a round-trip ticket to Alaska and Hawaii isn't to be taken lightly). The biggest benefit is the time and energy it will save you in your search for a position. SCA does all of the legwork for you. They track down the positions in parks and forests all over the country and list them in a catalog that you receive as part of the application package. The listings are short on color, but they're sufficient to give you a general idea of what you would be doing and whether you qualify. Below, are two sample listings from SCA's Fall 1988 catalog:

GRAND CANYON NATIONAL PARK
Interpretive Assistant: will assist with the daily opera-
tion of the visitor center and related public programs,
conduct public programs on the natural and human his-
tory of Grand Canyon, 40 percent; assist visitors at the
information desk, 45 percent; and participate in routine
work assignments related to running a large visitor cen-
ter operation in a large National Park, 15 percent. Vol-
unteer will be working in a very visible public contact
uniformed position. Desire: background in natural or
human history, recreation or forestry either through
work experience or college; good speaking skills. Per-
sonal transportation required.

MOAB DISTRICT, SAN JUAN RESOURCE AREA
(Bureau of Land Management)
Duties include: provide information and assistance to
visitors and recreation users in the Grand Gulch Plateau
Management Area and Dark Canyon Primitive Area, 50
percent; conduct vehicle, foot and horseback patrols of
the Grand Gulch Primitive Area and Cedar Mesa, 25
percent; perform maintenance duties such as painting,
trail clearing and general facility maintenance, 25 per-
cent. Independent project possible. Require: valid driv-
er's license; ability to work alone in remote and isolated
areas; ability to interact in a positive manner with all
types of people. Desire: background in recreation or cul-
tural management, environmental awareness, and inter-
pretation. Personal transportation recommended.

As part of your application process (the application itself is fairly straightforward), you choose four positions that appeal to you most. SCA staff members evaluate your choices and send your application on to the supervisor of the position for which you are either best suited or have the best shot of acquiring. The supervisor makes the final decision. If all choices are out of reach or have already been filled, the SCA, with your consent, will steer you to another position.

Working through SCA, you won't have to call volunteer coordinators in far-off ranger stations in Alaska, Hawaii, Wyoming, or California, to find out that the position you have your heart set on has already been filled. You also don't have to negotiate your room and board arrangement because all SCA positions guarantee adequate accommodations and a minimum weekly stipend of $40 (not to mention the free transportation). Most significantly, the SCA patch on your button-down shirt gives you some credibility and backing. You won't have to worry about winding up on a maintenance chain gang.

Conveniences notwithstanding, there are some disadvantages to working through the SCA's program. First, you hear only about a small percentage of the thousands of available positions. Granted, SCA doesn't bother with such drudge jobs as fire watcher (where you sit in a tower and keep a lookout for forest fires), but they also miss some interesting ones.

In addition, the SCA Resource Assistant Program is getting more competitive, especially during the summer months. The program is an enclave for budding foresters, botanists, wilderness specialists, and others. The applicants with practical college majors and plans for graduate school have a competitive edge for the preferred jobs, such as wildlife research positions and the ones based in Hawaii and Alaska.

Basic liberal arts graduates shouldn't give up on SCA,

but you need to be savvy in choosing from the catalog listings. SCA lists a good number of interpretation (education)
and recreation jobs that usually don't call for any expertise.
And they also list opportunities in some of the more obscure
national and state lands that are perfectly beautiful but
attract less attention than the biggies like Yellowstone and
Yosemite. So if you lack the serious experience, set your
sights on one of the less specialized positions in one of the
lesser known places. "I was limited in what I was qualified
for because I had more humanities than science," says
Molly, who got her job at Baxter State Park [Maine]
through the SCA. "But there were plenty of positions like
the interpretation programs. And for those, you don't need
four years of forestry to be good. You just need a willingness
to learn and to deal with the public."

METHOD 2

American Hiking Society
1015 31st Street, NW
Washington, D.C. 20007
(202) 385-3252

Helping Out in the Outdoors is a simple staple-bound
booklet that won't win any awards for design, and its two-
column, single-spaced format isn't terribly inviting, but it's
crammed with over a thousand volunteer opportunities in
national, state, and private lands throughout America, and

it's absolutely invaluable to someone looking for an expense-paid volunteer position. In putting this publication together twice a year, the American Hiking Society performs an outstanding service. Not only will it spare you incalculable amounts of time and effort, but it will expose you to positions in tiny sites or obscure districts of minor agencies and wonderful jobs in beautiful settings that you would not be able to find on your own. Take, for example, the following listing from the Fall/Winter 87/88 catalog for a position in a small state-run recreation area in Wyoming:

WYOMING RECREATION COMMISSION, STATE PARKS AND HISTORIC SITES: PINEDALE DISTRICT
Beautiful mountains, high lakes, alpine vegetation in the Bridger Wilderness. WILDERNESS RANGER needed June-Sept. Benefits include $7/day, training, supervision. WILDERNESS INFORMATION specialist stationed in back-country residence near trailhead to contact entering visitors. Some trail patrol. Benefits include $7/day, A-frame or log cabin housing, supervision, training. Contact: Elizabeth Ballard, Pinedale Ranger District, P.O. Box 220, Pinedale, WY 82941. Phone: 307/ 367-4326

The AHS invites over eight hundred different agencies—national, state, regional, and private—to list their volunteer staff needs in each semiannual issue of *Helping Out in the Outdoors*. Some of the agencies decline this offer, but the number of available options listed are still overwhelming. This is the one downside aspect of pursuing the job search by yourself. You must approach *Helping Out in the Outdoors* with a clear idea of what you want to do and where you want to go. Otherwise, you will get carried away

by the preponderance of opportunities and likely rack up a
five-hundred-dollar phone bill merely chatting with different volunteer coordinators and supervisors around the
country who are all (in my experience) very interesting and
quite talkative.

On the other hand, once you narrow down your choices to
a reasonable number, I can't overstate the importance of
talking personally with the supervisors. "You learn more
from one phone call than you will in ten letters," says California's Jim Eicher. These people will supply the details of
the experience—the beautiful cabin, where to get a bear
bell so you won't startle a grizzly as you explore a new trail,
the best bar in the nearby town. What's more, you'll know
pretty quickly whether you would want to work for that
person, information that is well worth an inflated phone
bill.

METHOD 3

WORKING IN THE FAMOUS PARKS

The big-name national parks don't always list their volunteer opportunities with the Student Conservation Association or in *Helping Out in the Outdoors*. Scores of people
dream of working in these parks, and their volunteer programs simply don't need the additional publicity.

But America's high profile parks—the Yosemites, Yel-
lowstones, and Grand Canyons—have thriving volunteer
programs to help their seasonal staffs cope with the millions of tourists tramping through every year. And while
getting positions here is competitive, you have a fair
chance of finding an opening if you apply early enough. For

the peak season that runs from May through September, for instance, it is advisable to send your application in before the previous Christmas.

The best way to find out about the options at a given park is by calling the volunteer coordinator. I found them easy to reach through the park's main number. Make sure the coordinator understands that you want an expense-paid volunteer program with housing, and that you're not a local resident volunteering for a few days a week.

The following list includes Ameria's most popular parks (as measured by yearly tourist traffic), plus some of the more exotic parks and those most often recommended by veteran outdoor travelers. All of these have active volunteer programs.

ACADIA NATIONAL PARK, Maine: (207) 288-3338

Flanked by one of the country's most dramatic rocky coast lines, New England's only national park is over 40,000 acres of chilly lakes, grand peaks, and serene forests. It is also within a short drive of some of Maine's tourist hubs.

BADLANDS NATIONAL PARK, South Dakota: (605) 433-5361

The Sioux, who once dominated the plains, called this arid stretch of South Dakota Mako Sico, or "bad lands," for its unearthly stubble of crumbly land formations. Today, nearly a million tourists visit each year for its dramatic views and unusual wildlife and one of the world's largest collection of mammal fossils—skeletons and footprints of the three-toed horses, saber-toothed tigers and oversized relatives of sheep, camels, and other animals that roamed here 25 million years ago.

DENALI NATIONAL PARK and PRESERVE, Alaska: (907) 683-2294

In 1980, Mount McKinley National Park gained over four million acres and a new name. With McKinley still the centerpiece of this six-million-acre park (Denali is the Aleutian word for "the high one"), its six million acres hold a cache of glaciers and lakes, tundra and forests, and a population of animals that includes grizzlies, dall sheep, and caribou. Though Denali's volunteer program is more active than that of any other national park in Alaska, it doesn't compare to those of the large parks in the lower 48 states.

GRAND CANYON, Arizona: (602) 638-7888

Incomparable to those who have seen it, this 1,218,375-acre park encompasses a kaleidoscope of life zones, climates, wildlife and plant life.

GLACIER NATIONAL PARK, Montana: (406) 888-5441

Snowy glaciers, remnants of the last ice age, melt into waterfalls that tumble into clear lakes. Fields of wildflowers, congregations of eagles, grizzlies, and horned white mountain goats, forests of towering Western Red Cedar, and two ranges of the Rocky Mountains are some of the more magnificent sites in this million-acre-plus park.

GREAT SMOKY MOUNTAINS NATIONAL PARK, North Carolina-Tennessee: (615) 436-5615

Straddling the border of North Carolina and Tennessee, this luxuriant park attracts more visitors than any other in the United States. It is crisscrossed by trails (including seventy miles of the Appalachain Trail) and six hundred miles of streams. Try to be here in early April during the spectacular burst of wildflower fields.

HALEAKALA NATIONAL PARK, Maui, Hawaii: (808) 572-9306

The park extends from the "lunar"-scape of Haleakala volcano to an impassably dense rain forest to the flower-strewn Hana coast. And despite its isolation, it is one of the most sought-after volunteer spots.

OLYMPIC NATIONAL PARK, Washington: (206) 452-4501

The shoreline, rain forest, and mountain ranges of this park are beautiful. But the special feature of this park is its goat relocation program. Hundreds of the terrain-damaging varmints are being stalked, tranquilized, and transported back to a wilderness preserve in their native Utah. The cost: $1,000 to $1,500 per goat.

ROCKY MOUNTAIN NATIONAL PARK, Colorado: (303) 586-2371

The southern Rocky Mountains are bighorn sheep territory, 417 square miles of dense woods, glacier-cut streams, and rugged summits. Three hundred and fifty miles of hiking trails attract over half a million hikers each year. (Denver is only two hours away.)

YELLOWSTONE NATIONAL PARK, Wyoming: (307) 344-7381

America's oldest, and arguably its most famous national park. Still, the park service has worked hard to keep most of the area in pristine shape, with a major wildlife refuge (for bear, elk, moose and bighorn sheep, to name a few), a waterfall twice as high as Niagara, over a thousand miles of trails, and dozens of geysers (including Old Faithful).

YOSEMITE NATIONAL PARK, California: (209) 372-0200

The peaks and valleys of the Sierra Nevadas make this 1,189-square-mile park a year-round playground for Californians and a preserve for a varied wilderness that is both striking and harmonious. It is also the site of a forest of Giant Sequoia trees, the largest living things on earth.

MORE ABOUT YOUR JOB SEARCH

Each park, forest, and recreation area has different features that will have an impact on your experience. Being a campground host at Yellowstone National Park, with its annual parade of two million tourists, is a totally different experience from being a campground host at the remote Alsea Falls recreation site in Oregon, where there are four staff members and room for about sixteen tents. The responsibilities are much the same—helping campers get settled, collecting fees, answering questions, and keeping the place orderly. But the realities of the two experiences have little in common, in much the same way that a waiter at a Texas barbecue joint will have a totally different experience from that of a waiter at an elegant French restaurant in Manhattan. Their tasks are the same but their ambience and clientele bear little resemblance to each other.

Since the most common volunteer positions are available in hundreds of different settings, it's in your best interest

to figure out whether you'll be happier in a vast multifaceted park like Glacier or Yosemite, a scenic desert like
Mesa Verde or Canyon Lands, or a relatively unknown historical and archaeologcial site like the Pueblo ruins at New
Mexico's Chaco Culture National Park historical site. Each
geographic area has its own recreational and scenic rewards. If you love canoeing, you might as well end up in
one of the hundreds of places with hospitable lakes and
rivers. If you are a painter who is inspired by desert sun-
sets, you could head to Utah's Bryce Canyon National Park,
Arizona's Petrified Forest National Park, or any number of
other sites scattered throughout the arid portions of Utah,
New Mexico, Colorado, and Arizona. If you want to be near
a big city, there are dozens of opportunities in the National
Park Service's Golden Gate district outside of San Francisco.

Aside from basic geography, the two factors that will set
the pace of your experience are the size of the park staff
and the tourist flow. All of the high-profile parks—the Yel-
lowstones, Yosemites, Grand Canyons, Lake Tahoes—attract upward of one million visitors a year and have large
seasonal staffs of career rangers, seasonal workers, and volunteers. These parks also tend to have ample social opportunities. "We have a great time up here," says Valerie, the
volunteer coordinator at Badlands National Park. Smaller
parks with fewer tourists tend to have skeletal staffs, so
unless you're content with peace and quiet, expect to seek
your fun in nearby towns.

THE LAND MANAGEMENT AGENCIES

Most of the expense-paying volunteer positions are sponsored by the federal agencies that manage much of the open
land in this country: The National Park Service, The U.S.

Forest Service, and the Bureau of Land Management. Each of these agencies has a different land management philosophy and a different perspective to offer their volunteers. Understanding these variations can help you decide to which stretch of forest, park, beach, or mountain to apply your energies.

The National Park Service is a preservation agency. Its mandate is to ensure that areas of great ecological, historic and scenic importance—from the Grand Canyon to the seashore of Cape Cod to the laboratory of Thomas Edison— stay as they are, forever. "So for someone who is most interested in conservation," says Jim Eicher, an agency outdoor recreation planner in California, "the National Park Service has the most to teach."

The U.S. Forest Service and the Bureau of Land Management, on the other hand, are mixed-use agencies. They are attuned to the conservation and preservation of their lands, and they, too, have campgrounds, trails, and wilderness reserves like the National Park Service. But unlike the Park Service, these agencies are in the timber, gas, oil, and mineral business. They lease forest lands to timber companies, their grazing fields to cattle rangers, and their rich mineral deposits to gas and oil companies. So if you're interested in learning how the elimination of an old-growth forest will affect a population of spotted owls, or have your sights set on eventually working for an oil company, these agencies might be worth considering.

For more information:

- **Bureau of Land Management**
  Office of Public Affairs
  18th and C Streets, N.W.
  Room 5600
  Washington, D.C. 22042
  (202) 343-5717

- **National Park Service
  Office of Public Affairs
  18th and C Street, N.W.
  Room 3424
  Washington, D.C. 22042
  (202) 343-7394**

- **U.S. Forest Service
  P.O. Box 090
  Washington, D.C. 20090
  (202) 447-3957**

RECOMMENDED READING

The National Park Guide, by Michael Frome. Formerly published by Rand McNally, this most comprehensive book lists all 337 sites within the National Park Service. Color photos and poetic articles by a veteran outdoorsman and travel writer and plenty of maps make this book the best basic guide on the market. Another worthwhile purchase by the same author is *America's Favorite Parks,* now also published by Prentice-Hall. It's available at most travel bookstores and libraries.

The Sierra Club Guides to the National Parks. These five books reveal America's national parks through incomparable photography and articles written by a team of expert naturalists. Each volume of these beautifully designed books covers a different region of the country. Packed with information ranging from geological and human history to the number of campgrounds, these books are well worth the price. Published by Stewart, Tabori & Chang, distributed by Random House, and available at most travel and sporting bookstores—or through the Sierra Club ($14.95 per volume, The Sierra Club, 730 Polk Street, San Francisco, California 94109; (415) 776-2211).

HIKING THE APPALACHIAN TRAIL

> **Appalachian Trail Conference**
> P.O. Box 807
> Harpers Ferry, West Virginia 25425
> (304) 535-6331

The Appalachian Trail is the longest marked footpath in the world. For 2,100 miles it winds from Georgia to Maine through some of the most rugged and beautiful territory of the South and New England. Every year, more than a thousand men and women of all ages and backgrounds quit their jobs, sell their cars, give up their apartments, and with their lives strapped to their backs, set out to hike the trail. Tens of thousands have tried since the trail was completed in 1938, and only slightly more than 1,500 have succeeded.

But despite the odds, hiking the Appalachian Trail, or A.T. as it's called by serious hikers, is a classic post-graduate undertaking. It is a chance to reflect on yourself and to get in touch with the natural environment. And even if you don't finish the journey, you will come away with a core of self-reliance, self-awareness and understanding that you'll carry with you for the rest of your life. "It can change your life," says Cindy Ross, a veteran thru-hiker and author of the widely read *A Woman's Journey,* which chronicles her experiences on the trail. "Even if you have a [hiking] partner, you have five or six months, sixteen hours a day that you are with your own thoughts. You think about all sort of things: your past, present and future, your dreams, what screwed up and what went well. Just being with yourself for all that time lets you see who you are. You don't solve all your problems. But you come away accepting yourself. You know more about what makes you happy and what you want out of your life."

Your trip will begin some time close to April 1, and should end by October 1, although you should try to finish up by mid-September to avoid snow in the mountains. People have hiked the trail in under 90 days ("Young single men like to go fast," says Cindy). But a more enjoyable time frame is five or six months, at an average pace of twelve or thirteen miles a day. This allows you to take frequent days off to explore the wilderness around the trail and to take civilization breaks in the towns that crop up along the way. "Getting up in the morning to hike the trail isn't like getting up to go to work," says Susan Henley, the project director for the Appalachian Trail Conference and veteran thru-hiker. "I felt a sense of freedom on the trail, I could do what I wanted to. If I didn't feel like hiking, I didn't. And if I felt like hiking 25 miles because it was a gorgeous day and I felt great, then I did."

The south-to-north route is the preferred course, as spring hits the South early and unwinds slowly as you head North. And heading out from Georgia in early April puts you on a collision course with the spectacular spring bloom in North Carolina, Tennessee, and Virginia—days on end of brilliant wildflowers like lady slippers, azaleas, mountain laurel, and iris. "In south central Virginia, it was like walking through a beautiful garden for four days straight," says Susan.

Including equipment, the journey will cost you between $1,500 and $2,000, although some people get away with spending as little as $600 and many spend much more. Food is the main expense, but seemingly small considerations like laundry, postage, and souvenirs add up quickly. Extra funding will buy you more convenience and comfort —some hotel stays, more lavish meals in town—but money doesn't have a significant affect on your quality of life. The trail is not the place to cultivate gourmet tastes. Food must be lightweight, nonperishable, and uncrushable. Fresh fruits and vegetables don't carry well, uncanned meats spoil, and breads turn to dust from the pressure of your pack. "We used to stomp on our bread before we packed it so we wouldn't be surprised and disappointed when we opened it later," says David, who hiked the trail with his brother Warren. Even the most health conscious usually succumb to a shameless junk food regime to satisfy big appetites, consuming favorites such as dried pasta ensembles like macaroni and cheese and Ramen Noodles, Pop Tarts, instant oatmeal, cookies, candies, snack cakes, peanut butter carried in Ziplock bags, processed cheese and crackers, and the occasional can of stew, Vienna sausages, tuna or spreadable meat. "We had a friend who did a scientific study of the best trail food, based on nutrition and weight. He found that sunflower seeds were the best," says David. "But we saw him a little later, and he told us to forget sunflower seeds. He was stuffing himself with cookies and candy." Junk food notwithstanding, the trail promotes great health, and unless you drink some bad water along the way (a preventable occurrence) you will emerge in prime physical condition.

As an AT thru-hiker, you become a member of a "mobile

community," as David puts it. If you choose the popular south-to-north route and set out around April 1, you will be in the orbit of hundreds of other hikers. Most people spend the days hiking alone or with a partner and meet up with other hikers at night. "I started out because I loved the outdoors," says Susan. "But as it ended up, the people were the most special thing about the trip."

This community is tight-knit, and though you might never meet some of the hikers ahead of you and behind you, you'll almost certainly hear about them and they'll hear about you. Relationships form quickly and gain momentum on the trail and most hikers finish with a new cadre of lifelong friends. Warren and David, for instance, hiked with a retired telephone company worker whose trail name was June Dreamer. ("We thought he planned to finish the trail in June," says Warren, "but it turned out that June is his wife's name.") After about three hundred miles, June Dreamer fell sick and had to pack up and head home to Connecticut. "He called our father to find out when we would be on the trail in Connecticut," says Warren. "He drove to the trail and looked for us. Amazingly enough, he found us, drove us 60 miles back to his house, fed us, put us up, and drove us 60 miles back to the trail the next day."

The thru-hiking society has its own customs and traditions. Each hiker, for instance, is known to other hikers by his or her trail name. Warren and David were famous as the Blues Brothers ("Everything we had on was blue," says Warren). Others on the trail that year included Rattler, Madman, the Flack Packers, Hiker Bob, Flash, and Hot Flash.

The social hubs along the trail are the two hundred shelters that spring up every twelve miles or so. These rustic, three-sided dwellings are welcome protection from cold, rainy nights and storms. Vibrant community centers, they accommodate anywhere between six and eighteen people. Floor space is available—but first come, first served. If you arrive too late to lay your sleeping bag down inside, there's usually a campsite just outside (trail custom dictates that there is always room for one more in bad weather).

Shelters help bind the trail community together; it's there that information is traded, advice is sought, friendships are sealed, and perhaps most important to solitary hikers, where experiences are shared. "It's really nice to be able to tell someone about your day on the trail," says Susan. "You tell each other about the gorgeous waterfall you saw, or the deer in the woods."

Of the many forms of communication along the trail ("Once someone left a note on the trail that said 'Rattler seen here, 12:15,' " says hiker Lori), the most interesting are the log books that hikers place in the shelters. Each time you pass through a shelter, you sign into the log book and offer your feelings, stories, and insights about the hike so far. One hiker, a talented cartoonist, expressed himself in pictures. The logs become the collective diary of the trail community, and in leafing through the log when you get to a shelter, you find clues as to the kind of personalities you'll encounter later in your journey. "You follow people through their log entries and when you finally meet up in a town it's like a big reunion," says Lori. "One guy wrote a short story bit by bit along the way."

The closeness of the community of thru-hikers takes some pressure off your decision of whether to hike alone or with a partner. If you set out alone and regret it, you can easily pick up a partner along the trail, or tag along with a large group. If you definitely want a hiking partner but can't find a taker among your friends, you might be able to link up with someone through the advertisements printed in the back pages of the *Appalachian Trailway News,* the bi-monthly magazine published by the Appalachian Trail Conference.

The trail isn't a dangerous place, but there are some inherent natural risks—slippery rocks, extreme cold, sudden storms, stomped snakes—that are better confronted as a team. And there have been a handful of violent incidents in the past few years, mostly near towns. Officially, the Appalachian Trail Conference discourages solo hiking. But they also acknowledge that scores of people do it. "We're less worried about the thru-hikers because of the social network," says Brian King, an ATC spokesperson. "They keep track of each other."

If you choose to hike with a close friend, girlfriend, or boyfriend, bear in mind that the trail is a constant test. It will either tear you apart or bind you together for good. Countless marriages have melted in the heat of Pennsylvania, dissolved during a week of relentless drizzle, or simply disintegrated under the pressure of spending 24 hours a day together. "Most romantic couples that start out together don't end together," says Lori. Other relationships, however, blossom. Cindy, for one, met her husband on the trail. And the hiking experience sealed the bond between brothers Warren and David. "My brother and I were never very close together," says Warren. "But on the trail, we were never separated for more than ten minutes. We are very different types and we fought like cats and dogs. But we really got to know each other. And getting to know my brother was one of the best things about the trip. We're really tight now."

The scenic, social, and individually valuable marvels of the trail are countless. But they don't always come easily. And veteran thru-hikers warn against the danger of approaching the trail with overly romantic notions. As Cindy points out, hiking the AT is not a vacation. It is an alternative existence, with an appropriate spectrum of highs and lows. "In real life, it's easy to shelter yourself from the hard times," says Cindy. "On the trail, you can't. You can't say, 'Shit, it's raining, I'm going into the house.' You have to deal with what's in front of you. I never thought I could have done something like that. But since I have the accomplishment under my belt, I feel that I can try anything."

As for physical demands, there are some things to con-

sider. You will be hiking through some formidable mountain ranges—the Smokies that straddle the border of
Tennessee and North Carolina, the Whites in New Hampshire and the Mahoosucs in Maine. And there are times
when you'll be shimmying through rock clusters and climb-
ing hills with your hands. Not to mention the weather,
which can deliver days on end of rain, freezing mornings,
sudden snows and scorching afternoons. And don't forget
that you will be carrying your life on your back—months'
worth of clothes, tools, supplies, maps, and other essentials.
Even ascetics have trouble keeping their pack weight down
to the optimum twenty-five to thirty pounds, although after
a few days of lugging the equivalent of a pudgy child on
your back for a few days most people pare down their pack
and send the extras home. "You realize pretty fast what
you need and what you don't need when you have to carry
it all," says David, who dumped about twenty pounds on
the third day.

No amount of planning or practice will guarantee that
you will finish the trail. There are people who plan the trip
for two years, whip themselves into triathlon shape, and
don't last twenty miles. Others hit the trail with no hiking
experience and a pack-a-day smoking habit, and make it to
Maine in four months. Most people who give up do so within
the first ninety miles.

The best way to determine whether you are ready to challenge the trail is to head to the woods for a week or two. "If
you can backpack a week straight by yourself or with a
partner," says Cindy, "then you are capable of distances.
Because hiking the trail is just a series of week-long hikes.
If you are not comfortable with yourself in the woods for a
week, then you will not be able to handle five months."

As far as physical conditioning goes, thru-hikers agree
that anyone in reasonable shape can make this trip. Many
hikers after all, are well beyond retirement age. But bear
in mind that even if you are in top shape, you are probably

in for some achy nights during the first week or two. "Your legs are sore, and your back takes time to get used to the pack," says David. Veteran thru-hikers recommend maintaining a slow pace for the first couple of weeks and to take frequent breaks in town. "After a couple of weeks, anybody's body can handle the trail," says Cindy.

Equipment is subject to your own personal taste and needs. The basics include a warm sleeping bag (mummy style), a foam pad, a tarp or mosquito netting, a sturdy pair of boots (broken in before you leave), a roomy, comfortable pack, a portable stove and utensils, rain gear, and a first-aid kit. Many hikers do without a tent, saving themselves about five to ten pounds of pack weight but resolving themselves to some soggy nights if they reach a shelter after it's full. If you're not brand conscious, stick to basic equipment, and shop around a bit, you should be able to set yourself for under $300. Many people stick to army surplus and do it for much less. But there are, as you can imagine, countless opportunities to indulge in designer gortex raingear, elaborate water filter systems, and bar-mitzvah capacity tents. It's a question of your own style.

The best way to start planning your trip is by making inquiries at the Appalachian Trail Conference (ATC), the organization that maintains the trail. Their staff, which includes many veteran thru-hikers, will help you in every phase of planning the trip, from a recommended brand of hiking boots to a recommended restaurant that would make a nice spot to meet your parents during the way. They also stock the trail bibles and guides (see page 215).

SUMMARY

What it is: The Appalachian Trail, the longest marked footpath in the world, winds from Georgia to Maine for over 2,100 miles.

Opportunities for Recent Graduates: Hiking the entire length of the Appalachian Trail is a classic postgraduate experience.

Time Frame: The journey takes anywhere from three to seven months, depending on your pace. Most people take between five and six months, doing it from early April to October.

How Much it Costs: You can equip yourself for as little as $300. On the trail, you will need between $1,500 and $2,000, mostly for food and incidental expenses.

Requirements: You need a strong motivation to finish the trail and a relish for life in the outdoors. You should have long-distance back-packing experience and be in reasonable physical shape, although the first few weeks of hiking the trail will whip you into condition.

How to Prepare: The best way to prepare and gauge your readiness is to take at least one week-long back-packing trip either alone or with a friend. The Appalachian Trail Conference will help you plan the more practical aspects of the trip, such as what equipment you need, how to set your pace, and how to keep your pack-weight down. You should also read the trail bibles: *The Philosophers Guide, the Appalachian Hiker II,* and

A Woman's Journey (appropriate for men too). See below for book information.

Pros:

- Inspires great self-reliance and confidence.

- Camaraderie of the thru-hiking community.

- Beautiful natural environment.

- Simple life-style

Cons:

- Unpredictable weather.

- Stretches of rough terrain.

- Most people do not finish the journey.

RECOMMENDED READING

The following books are available through the Appalachian Trail Conference, P.O. Box 807, Harpers Ferry, West Virginia 25425-0807; (304) 535-6331.

A Woman's Journey, by Cindy Ross. This handwritten book contains an honest, moving account of the author's two-part thru-hike, illustrated with her charcoal sketches. Though it contains some practical advice, she focuses on the emotional issues ($7.95).

The Appalachian Hiker II, be Edward B. Garvey. The most famous book written by the trail's most beloved thru-hiker, this is *the* comprehensive guide to hiking the Appalachian Trail. Garvey covers virtually every practical and philosophical aspect of hiking the trail, including mileage charts, names and addresses of outfitters and mountain clubs, and even his favorite granola recipe ($9.95).

The 1988 Philosophers Guide. This tiny booklet contains everything you need to know about preparing for the hike, plus a blow-by-blow guide to towns, water sources, hostels, great restaurants, friendly townspeople, equipment shops, and anything else you might possibly need along the way. The information comes straight from the mouths of thru-hikers. Indispensable ($4.95).

FOR MORE INFORMATION

As a final note, mention should be made of other potential year-off options and opportunities excluded from previous chapters. I refrained from selecting professional internships and study abroad programs, abroad, for example, since they are so vast and varied that they deserve books of their own (which, in fact, have already been written). Other opportunities, like research expeditions and archaeological digs, which didn't quite fit the criteria, since participation might actually last only a few weeks. But some of these opportunities are so interesting that they may merit future reference. So here is a select list of resources that will help you do some research on your own.

INTERNSHIPS

An internship, whether in theater, medicine, writing, or banking, is an ideal way to try out your field of interest and to log some solid work experience. There are tens of thousands of internships available, each with its own set of benefits and requirements. Some are quite structured, pay high salaries, and offer substantial responsibilities. Others rely more on individual initiative and assertiveness. The following two books include annually updated lists and brief descriptions of internships available in the United States and in some foreign countries:

1989 Internships: 38,000 On-the-Job Training Opportunities For College Students and Adults, edited by Katherine Jobst ($21.95, Writers Digest Books, 1507 Dana Avenue, Cincinnati, Ohio 45207; (800) 543-4644; in Ohio, (800) 551-0884).

The National Directory of Internships, edited by Sally Migliore ($23, National Society for Internships and Experiential Education, 3509 Haworth Drive, Suite 207, Raleigh, North Carolina, 27609; (919) 787-3263).

STUDYING ABROAD

A well–structured study program abroad offers a supportive, intellectual framework for an overseas experience. And many, if not most, are open to recent graduates. You can either apply directly to a foreign institution through an American college, or through any number of independent sponsoring organizations. In each case, you should carefully evaluate the quality of the program. The following books and organizations will help you do so.

Academic Year Abroad, 1988–89, Edited by Edrice Howard. This book, published by the Institute of International

Education, lists more than 1,250 overseas study programs offered by American universities and colleges ($19.95, Institute of International Education, 809 United National Plaza, New York, New York 10017).

Council on International Educational Exchange
Study-abroad expert is one of many hats worn by this leader in student travel and related affairs. CIEE is involved in several academic programs in the USSR, France, China, Spain, and other countries, and it publishes books and studies on different aspects of the study-abroad experience. There are more than 30 CIEE offices around the world. For further information, contact the New York headquarters at 205 East 42 Street, New York, New York 10017, or call (212) 661-1414.

Directory of Programs in Soviet and East European Studies, 1987–1989. Put together by the American Association for the Advancement of Slavic Studies, this book includes information about more than two-hundred programs, degree and non-degree ($25, Encina Commons, Stanford University, Stanford, California 94305-6029).

National Committee on United States-China Relations
This organization publishes an annual list of academic programs in China. Available free of charge. (777 United National Plaza, New York, New York 10017-3521, (212) 922-1385).

Work Study Travel Abroad: The Whole World Handbook 1988–1989, by Marjorie Adoff Cohen with the Council on International Educational Exchange. A cache of useful information and advice on many types of overseas experiences, including study-abroad programs ($8.95, Council on International Educational Exchange, 205 East 42 Street, New York, New York 10017; (212) 661-1414).

ARCHAEOLOGICAL DIGS

There are hundreds of archaeological digs going on around the world. Right now, for instance, teams are excavating Islamic houses from the Middle Ages in Syria, studying gravestone inscriptions in Gibraltar, exploring a 19th century iron and steel company in New York, and unearthing a Gallo-Roman villa in the French Alps.

Many archaeological teams take on volunteers with no previous experience to help in all facets of the field work. The work is often hard and exacting—digging, sifting, surveying, cataloguing. But you can learn a great deal about the culture you are exploring and about archaeological methods in general. In some cases, you can also receive academic credit.

Most volunteer positions come up in the summer months, during the season's last several weeks. The costs vary dramatically, but the average hovers between $100 and $300 per week for expenses, plus the cost of traveling to the site.

The best source of information on archaeological digs is the *Archaeological Fieldwork Opportunities Bulletin,* published annually by the Archaeological Institute of America. The publication lists an expansive selection of digs scheduled in this country and around the world. Each listing includes information on volunteer opportunities, costs, and duties, plus short blurbs about the dig. The book, which costs $8, is available by mail from the Archaeological Institute of America, 675 Commonwealth Avenue, Boston, Massachusetts 02215; (617) 353-9361.

RESEARCH EXPEDITIONS

A number of non-profit research organizations invite volunteers to tag along on their scientific expeditions. Some of the trips are quite exotic. Some recent ventures, for instance, had volunteers excavating mummies in the desert of Chile, digging for fossils in a Masai village in Tanzania, exploring Eskimo ruins in the Alaskan bush, and exploring reef life off the coast of Cozumel, Mexico. These trips are highly praised by past volunteers, and are becoming increasingly popular vacation options for people who favor a productive diversion to lounging on a beach. You do not, in most cases, need any particular experience or expertise to sign on.

Conservation Education Diving Archaeology Museums (CEDAM)

CEDAM is a conservation-minded member organization involved with undersea research, exploration, and archaeology. This year, CEDAM members will be exploring the waters around the Fiji Islands, the Galapagos Islands, the Sea of Cortez, Belize, and other areas. The membership fee is $8 for students (under 25) (CEDAM International, Fox Road, Croton-on-Hudson, New York, New York 10520; (914) 271-5365).

Earthwatch

Earthwatch is a nonprofit organization that provides funding for biologists, anthropologists, archaeologists, and other scientists involved in field work around the world. They also assemble teams of volunteers to help those scientists. Most Earthwatch trips are between two and four weeks long, and cost between $500 and $1,500. (Earthwatch, 680 Mount Auburn Street, Box 403, Watertown, Massachusetts 02272; (617) 926-8200.)

Learning Vacations: The all-season guide to educational travel, by Gerson G. Eisenberg. This book catalogs a vast selection of short-term research trips, seminars, and other interesting offerings. It is available in travel bookstores ($9.95, Peterson Guides, Princeton, New Jersey).

University Research Expeditions Program
This program sends volunteers to assist University of California scholars in the field. But you do not have to be a UC student or graduate to participate. In addition to the science-oriented opportunities, like watching sea lions in Australia or studying Moroccan sheep, UREP's extensive catalog includes research forays into art, music and sociology. Last year, for instance, UREP participants studied the art of Peking Opera in China, jazz in Puerto Rico, and the education system in Great Britain. Most trips are held during the summer months, and last for two weeks (you have a choice of three different sessions). Costs average between $1,000 and $2,000, plus the cost of airfare to the trip assembly point (University of California, Berkeley, California 94720; (415) 642-6586).